An Introduction to
English Folk Song

An Introduction to
English Folk Song

MAUD KARPELES

London
OXFORD UNIVERSITY PRESS
New York   Toronto
1973

Oxford University Press, Ely House, London W.1

GLASGOW NEW YORK TORONTO MELBOURNE WELLINGTON
CAPE TOWN IBADAN NAIROBI DAR ES SALAAM LUSAKA ADDIS ABABA
DELHI BOMBAY CALCUTTA MADRAS KARACHI LAHORE DACCA
KUALA LUMPUR SINGAPORE HONG KONG TOKYO

ISBN 0 19 313125 0

© Oxford University Press 1973

Printed in Great Britain by Richard Clay (The Chaucer Press), Ltd., Bungay, Suffolk

Contents

Preface

This book, as its title implies, is not addressed to scholars who are seeking to advance their studies, but to those who have been attracted by the songs and would like to find out more about them. I hope in particular that it will be of use to students and teachers.

A great deal has been written about folk song and to add yet another book may seem redundant, but my aim has been to set up a few signposts that will indicate some of the roads and by-paths that may be followed in search of further knowledge and enjoyment of this inexhaustible subject.

What is folk music? How has it been perpetuated? What are its dominant characteristics? And what is its role in the life of today? These are some of the questions I shall discuss though I am aware that I shall leave much unanswered. We can probe and delve as we may, but in folk song as in other arts there will always remain mysteries which cannot readily be explained.

Folk song can be studied from many points of view: from that of musicology, literary criticism, sociology, and so on. These studies will all throw light on the subject, but a real appreciation of folk song can only be obtained through its practice and through the aesthetic emotions which it arouses. Folk music, though it has distinctive qualities, is yet part of the great world of music, which Vaughan Williams has described as 'the reaching out to ultimate realities by means of ordered sound'.

The first authoritative book on English folk song was Cecil Sharp's *English Folk Song: Some Conclusions*, which was originally published in 1907 and went through four editions, the fourth (1965) being edited by the present writer. This edition, which is now out of print, has been published in facsimile by

E. P. Publishing Ltd. The present book is based very largely on the views expressed by Cecil Sharp and I have quoted freely from his 'conclusions'. Indeed, it is impossible to avoid doing so. If the present 'Introduction' does no more than familiarize the reader with Cecil Sharp's epoch-making book I shall feel it has been worth while.

Another book to which I have constantly referred is Gordon Hall Gerould's *The Ballad of Tradition*, which gives a convincing exposition of the traditional processes which have gone into the making and moulding of folk songs. Gerould's *The Making of Ballads* (*Modern Philology* xxi, 1923), which formed the basis of his later work, was read by Cecil Sharp shortly before his death and he regarded it as 'the best thing that has been written on the subject'.

To Mr. Frank Howes I owe an apology for having used the same heading for Chapter 1 as he did in his *Folk-Music of Britain—and Beyond*. Actually, my chapter was drafted before his book appeared and, since the title describes the contents of the chapter better than any other I could think of, I have let it stand. In any case, I am glad to take this opportunity of drawing attention to this informative book, which should be read by all students of folk song.

There are several people to whom I have turned for help in the preparation of this book and I wish to acknowledge my gratitude to Professor B. H. Bronson, Dr. Francis Collinson, and Dr. Hugh Shields for information I have obtained from them. Others to whom I owe a deep debt of gratitude are Professor Peter Crossley-Holland and John Thomson, both of whom read a draft of the book and made many helpful suggestions. In fact, the book owes its existence, for good or for ill, to John Thomson who egged me on to write it.

Finally I would thank the members of the Oxford University Press who were connected with the production of the book for their invaluable help and advice.

London, 1972   *Maud Karpeles*

I

The Name and Nature of Folk Song

It is difficult to say when the term 'folk song' was first coined, but it seems to have been translated from the German word *Volkslied*, which was brought into use by Herder in the second half of the eighteenth century.[1] To give a name is one thing, but to define the named object is another, and for nearly two hundred years the parentage and nature of folk song have given rise to fierce controversy which is not even yet completely silenced.[2] As Goethe, himself a collector of folk songs, said: 'We are always invoking the name of folk song without knowing quite clearly what we mean by it.' And that, probably, is even truer today than it was in Goethe's time.

The view, common among the early German Romantic writers, that folk song was a kind of mysterious, spontaneous product of the folk soul is summed up in Wilhelm Grimm's oft-quoted saying that the folk song 'dichtet sich selbst' (composes itself), a saying into which possibly more has been read than Grimm himself intended. Later scholars have rejected this nebulous theory, and many have claimed that the songs owe their origin to individual authorship.

The two main schools of thought can for convenience be called, after the manner of the Germans, the 'production' and the 'reception' theories. Those of the production school

---

[1] The term 'folk lore' was first used by W. J. Thoms in a letter to the *Athenæum* dated 22 August 1846.

[2] For a fuller treatment of the subject, see Cecil Sharp, *English Folk Song: Some Conclusions*; G. H. Gerould, *The Ballad of Tradition*; Walter Wiora, *European Folk Song* (Oxford University Press, 1966); and Margaret Dean-Smith, *A Guide to English Folk Song Collections* (Liverpool, 1954).

of thought maintain that only those songs that have originated with the folk are folk songs. Those of the reception
school hold that the origin is unimportant and that all songs
that have achieved a wide currency among the people can
be termed folk song. Both conceptions contain elements of
the truth, but they do not give first importance to the one
overriding factor on which the making, and the nature, of
folk music depends.

Folk music is essentially that which has been passed on by
word of mouth—or by living example, if it be instrumental
music or dance—which, for convenience sake, we call 'oral
transmission'. In its formative stage, folk music, unlike most
'composed music' (the French 'musique savante' is really
a better term), is unwritten music which St. Isidore, Arch-
bishop of Seville in the early seventh century, described as
'music in which the sounds perish unless they are held within
the memory of man'.

Folk music has many analogies with language, and we
might remind ourselves that language was to a great extent
created by people who had not learned to read or write.
G. M. Trevelyan, in his *History of England* (pp. 131–2),
writes:

One outcome of the Norman Conquest was the making of the English
Language. As a result of Hastings, the Anglo-Saxon tongue . . . was
exiled from hall and bower, from court and cloister, and was despised
as a peasant's jargon. . . . It ceased almost . . . to be a written language.
The learned and the pedantic lost all interest in its forms, for the clergy
talked Latin and the gentry talked French. Now when a language is
seldom written and is not an object to scholars, it quickly adapts itself
in the mouths of plain people to the needs and uses of life. . . . During
the three centuries when our native language was a peasant's dialect
. . . it acquired the grace, suppleness and adaptability which are among
its chief merits.

The same might be said with equal truth of our folk
music. It is comparatively recently that it was written down
and came to the notice of musicians and scholars. Before that

there was a long period stretching into antiquity when it lived by oral transmission and in the 'memory of man', adapting itself as did language to the needs and uses of life.

Of the many definitions of folk music which have from time to time been put forward, the most satisfactory is probably that which was adopted by the International Folk Music Council at its conference at São Paulo in 1954. It runs thus:

Folk music is the product of a musical tradition that has been evolved through the process of oral transmission. The factors that shape the tradition are (i) continuity, which links the present with the past; (ii) variation, which springs from the creative impulse of the individual or the group; and (iii) selection by the community, which determines the form, or forms, in which the music survives.

To this definition the following more explicit statements were added:

(i) The term folk music can be applied to music that has been evolved from rudimentary beginnings by a community uninfluenced by popular or art music and it can likewise be applied to music which has originated with an individual composer and has subsequently been absorbed into the unwritten living tradition of a community;
(ii) The term does not cover popular composed music that has been taken over ready-made by a community and remains unchanged, for it is the refashioning and re-creation of the music by the community which gives it its folk character.

Continuity, variation, and selection: it will help us to understand the nature of folk song if we consider briefly how these three factors operate.

Continuity preserves the tradition. Indeed, as is self-evident, were there no element of continuity there could be no tradition. As examples of the persistence of tradition one has only to think of the many hundreds of folk songs that have migrated from the British Isles to the north American continent. Here are two similar versions of 'The Cuckoo', one from Bridgwater, Somerset, and the other from Grole Harbour, Newfoundland:

Ex. 1a

The— cuck-oo— 'is a fine— bird, ·She— sings— as she flies; She — brings— us good ti - dings, And tells—us no lies.

Ex. 1b

The— cuck-oo is a fine bird, She— sings— as she — flies; And the more she sings cuck-oo The— sum-mer draws nigh.

The following version with a different tune comes from the Kentucky Mountains:

Ex. 1c

The cuck-oo is a pret-ty bird, She sucks flowers so— sweet, She brings us sweet mu'-sic In·the Spring of—— the year.

Generally speaking, the texts have undergone less change than the tunes, though owing to the scarcity of records we can seldom trace the continued identity of a tune over a long period of time, even within its country of origin. It is easier to trace the text. A remarkable instance is given by Cecil Sharp: Mr. Henry Larcombe, a blind singer of eighty-two years of age living in Somerset, gave him a Robin Hood ballad consisting of eleven stanzas which were word for word almost the same as the corresponding stanzas in a black-letter broadside preserved in the Bodleian Library. Though the words of the ballad had been preserved elsewhere, they had never been produced in any form that could have reached country singers. Cecil Sharp therefore concluded that Mr. Larcombe's version had been preserved solely by oral tradition for two hundred years or more.[3]

Variation is responsible for the production of new forms. A song that lives by word of mouth is always to some extent in a state of flux. There is no printed notation to which it can be referred and by means of which it can be stereotyped. Thus in the nature of things there can be no single or correct version. Some versions are more pleasing than others, and that is all we can say. Each singer will repeat the song substantially as he learned it, but nearly always he will make slight variations which he introduces more or less unselfconsciously. Incidentally, he will always maintain that his is the 'correct' version, even though he may never sing the tune twice in exactly the same way. But this does not mean that the folk song grows in a haphazard way. Like language its development has been guided by certain principles which are none the less present because they are unconsciously held. The grammarian comes at a later stage and analyses the principles of language. He does not invent them.

But, it will be argued, a song must have had a beginning, and so surely the original (if we could find it) should be regarded as the correct version. In fact, it has been maintained by some who regard creative musical ability as the prerogative of the trained and educated musician that the manifold versions in which a folk song abounds are merely corruptions of the original composition due to the singer's loss of memory. Forgetfulness undoubtedly plays a part in oral transmission and many songs have suffered from it. But were forgetfulness the only cause of variation, how could we account for the existence side by side of two or more equally good but different versions of the same song? Of the following versions of 'The Unquiet Grave' who would

[3] See *English Folk Song: Some Conclusions*, pp. 22 and 28.

venture to say which was nearer to the original or which
showed signs of deterioration? As Gerould said, the singer
without skill in his craft has never 'stumbled into making
something beautiful through sheer forgetfulness'.

Ex. 2a

Ex. 2b

Cecil Sharp pointed out that the process whereby a folk
song is created is not fundamentally different from the
process employed by an individual creative artist. A musical
thought comes to the composer. He consciously works on
it, experiments, and develops it. It may take a few days or
many years before it reaches its final form. But there is this
difference between the two processes: whereas the evolution of the musical work of an individual composer is dependent upon one man (though even he is to some extent dependent on what has gone before) and is limited to his lifetime,
the evolution of a folk tune is dependent not on the one but

on the many. Its conception is a matter of many generations, and it never reaches its final form until the collector comes along; and even then it sometimes leads an independent existence apart from the printed page. Another difference is that the composer works consciously, whereas the changes made by the folk-song singer are more or less subconscious.

One has to remember that the folk singer is not tied to the printed page and so it is the idea of the tune, its general shape and feeling, that he wants to reproduce and not a series of fixed notes. And it is the same with the words.[4] The singer will not find it necessary to tell the story word for word as he got it, provided that he gives the sense of it. It is the small changes made by the singer that gradually lead to development and the emergence of new forms. As Cecil Sharp has said: 'The method of oral transmission is not merely one by which the folk song lives; it is a process by which it grows and by which it is created.'

One of the fascinations of collecting is to hear the same song from the lips of different singers, and it is an experience which helps one to understand the creative process. Cecil Sharp and I collected eighteen versions of 'Come all you fair and tender Ladies' in the Southern Appalachian Mountains and each one had differences. One of the simplest is this tune from Tennessee. It is straightforward, consisting of familiar phrases and following a rather obvious pattern:

---

[4] See Tristram P. Coffin, 'A description of Variation in the Traditional Ballad of America', in *The British Traditional Ballad in North America* (Philadelphia, 1963).

Ex. 3a

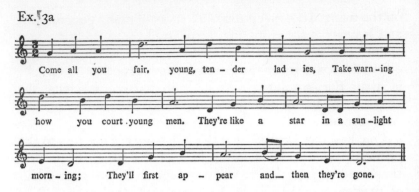

Come all you fair, young, ten - der lad - ies, Take warn - ing
how you court .young men. They're like a star in a sun - light
morn - ing; They'll first ap - pear and — then they're gone.

Then here are two more versions, from Kentucky and North Carolina respectively, each of which has some little touch or turn which enhances the rather bare statement of the first version:

Ex. 3b

Come all you fair and ten - der lad - ies, Take warn - ing
how you court young men. They're like a star in a sum - mer's
morn - ing; They'll first ap - pear and then they're gone.

Ex. 3c

If I had a known be - fore I'd a court - ed I nev - er
would have court - ed none; I'd have locked my — heart in a box of
gold - en and a fast - ened it up with a sil - ver pin.

And lastly, another from North Carolina, sung by Mrs. Reuben Hensley, which is not very different from the other versions, yet seems to stand apart (to my mind, at least) in the perfection of its artistry:

Ex. 3d

Come all ye fair and ten - der— la - dies, Be care - ful how you— court young men. They're like a star on a sum - mer's morn - ing; They'll first ap - pear and— then they're gone.

Had we found these different versions in the notebook of some great composer and not in Cecil Sharp's collection of folk songs we should regard them as interesting illustrations of the way in which a theme is developed in the mind of an artist. The analogy is apt, for in both cases it is the process of evolution that is at work, in one case operating through the consciousness of an individual, and in the other through the intuitive sense of untrained artists.

Roughly speaking, there are two types of traditional singers. There is the conservative type who will repeat the song more or less as he received it, and the other, the more imaginative type, who finds an outlet for his creative faculty by the modifications which he introduces, usually quite unconsciously, into the songs. Sometimes he will keep to the same tune throughout the song, but more often than not he will introduce variants in the successive stanzas. A good illustration of this is the singing of 'Fair Margaret and Sweet William' by Jeff Stockton of Tennessee.

Ex. 4

The evolution of folk song owes much to creative artists like Jeff Stockton and Mrs. Hensley. It is through their successive re-creations that new tunes emerge. It is not, however, these individual inventions alone that can determine the course of a folk song's development.

In the last resort *selection*, the third factor of evolution, has its say. A folk singer had until recently no means of recording his songs, and so unless they appealed to his fellows they would not be passed on. That means that the songs, or at any rate whatever in them was individual to that particular singer, would die with him unless they were adopted by other singers. In the long run the song is subject to the verdict of the community. The individual invents, but the community selects. And only those individual contributions are selected which reflect the feelings and the taste of the community. This selection is not, of course, a conscious concerted action of the community, but the result of acceptance or rejection by the individual members who make up the community.

Continuity, variation, selection: each process has a close bearing on the others and they are but different facets of tradition. The folk singer, though he may vary his song, does not exceed the bounds set by tradition; and selection by the community is also influenced by tradition. Thus continuity is maintained.

Folk music is a democratic art in the true sense of the word. Sir Hubert Parry put it well in his inaugural address to the Folk-Song Society in 1899:

True style comes not from the individual but from the products of the crowds of fellow-workers who sift and try and try again till they have found the thing that suits their native taste, and the purest product of such effort is folk-song.

The Relationship of Folk and Art Music

What type of people are, or were, responsible for the production of folk music? In other words, what do we mean by the 'folk'? Opinions differ.

To Béla Bartók the term folk music is synonymous with 'peasant music' and he defines the peasant class as 'that part of the population engaged in producing prime requisites and materials, whose need for expression, physical and mental, is more or less satisfied either with forms of expression corresponding to its own traditions, or with forms which, originating in a higher (urban) culture, have been instinctively altered so as to suit its own outlook and disposition.'[1]

Cecil Sharp's view coincided more or less with that of Bartók. He constantly speaks of folk song as peasant song, yet he denies that it is the sole prerogative of country people. (Incidentally, he himself noted a number of songs in London, though his informants may originally have been country people.) The real distinction, as he sees it, lies 'not between the music of the town and that of the country, but between that which is the product of the spontaneous and intuitive exercise of untrained faculties and that which is due to the conscious and intentional use of faculties especially cultivated and developed for the purpose'.[2]

In fact, folk songs have not infrequently been preserved by educated people. For instance, nearly all the songs in the famous collection of Looten and Feys, *Chants populaires*

[1] See *Hungarian Folk Music*, p. 1 (London, 1931).
[2] See *English Folk Song: Some Conclusions*, Ch. 1.

flamands (Bruges, 1879), were noted from a lady of good birth living at Bruges in 1795. In America, too, there are instances of educated persons who have had a large repertory of folk songs. And to come nearer home, we have only to think of Mrs. Brown of Falkland, who gave many beautiful ballads to Sir Walter Scott and Robert Jamieson (see p. 76)—though one must take into consideration that in Scotland there was formerly greater homogeneity of culture between the gentry and the peasantry than in England owing largely to the fact that all went to the same village school.[3]

However, it would be true to say that on the whole the folk-song tradition has thrived best among people living close to nature, bearing in mind, as Addison has said, that 'an ordinary ballad or song that is the delight of the common people cannot fail to please all such readers as are not unqualified for the entertainment by their affectation or ignorance'.[4]

Folk music does not live in a watertight compartment; and it has constantly been in touch with what, for want of a better word, we call art music (though this does not imply that folk music is without art). There have always been mutual influences and reciprocal borrowings. Ernest Closson, the great Belgian musicologist, has said with truth: 'Il arrive donc que lors qu'une mélodie d'art tombe dans la tradition, l'art ne fait que restituer au folklore ce qu'il lui avait lui-même emprunté.'[5]

To trace the many cross-currents that have, or may have, mutually influenced folk music and art music throughout the ages would be beyond the scope of this book, and we can give here only a few scattered examples and suggestions.

It must be remembered that before the adoption of the Guidonian system of notation at the beginning of the

3 See G. M. Trevelyan, *English Social History*, p. 426 (Longmans, London, 1942).
4 *The Spectator*, no. 70, 21 May 1711.
5 *Notes sur la Chanson Populaire en Belgique*, p. 55 (Brussels, 1913).

eleventh century most secular music was unwritten, so that in that respect there was no clear-cut distinction between folk music and composed music. Guido d'Arezzo was himself called *'inventor musicae'* (though it would probably be more accurate to say that he developed and popularized staff notation rather than that he invented it, as it was in existence before his day), and this may imply that in the popular mind the word 'music' was associated with the fixed and visible record of sound; a conception that exists even today, in that folk singers will sometimes speak of a song without a printed tune as a 'song without music'.

There is but little tangible evidence whereby we can determine the influence of ecclesiastical music on folk song, though it is reasonable to suppose that it existed. On the other hand, there are many instances of popular music being adopted or adapted for liturgical use.[6]

The relationship between the early Gregorian plainsong of the church and the popular music of the people is not easy to determine, but it is believed that the primitive elements of plainsong may have a common origin with those of folk song. However that may be, each has developed according to its respective needs. Though early plainsong, like folk song, was not written down, it was nevertheless subject to conscious codification and fixed rules, and the same is true of much Oriental music; whereas folk song knew no other restrictions than those imposed by natural selection.

In the Ambrosian hymn, the change from quantitative metre to stress rhythm for each successive stanza is held by some authorities to be due to the influence upon hymn writers of the popular Saturnine poetry of the day.[7]

In the motets and masses of the polyphonic period there are many examples of the borrowing of popular tunes to serve as *canti fermi*. One of the most famous was the French

---

[6] See R. Vaughan Williams, *National Music*, Ch. ix (Oxford University Press, London, 1924).

[7] See H. O. Hughes, *Latin Hymnody*, p. 7 (London, 1922).

or Provençal song tune, 'L'homme armé', and there was also our English melody, 'Westron Wynde', which was used by Taverner and others.

Popular tunes have also been put to religious use by being mated to psalms and hymns, the latter sometimes being a paraphrase of the secular song. One of the first to adopt this practice was Heinrich Laufenberg in Germany, who died in 1460. Fortunately for the interest of posterity he indicated the first words of the secular songs with which the tunes were associated, and a number have been identified as folk songs.[8] The practice was freely used at the time of the Reformation, and Martin Luther was among those who saw the value of setting hymns, or Chorals, to tunes that the people would know and wish to sing.

The custom of 'parodying' obtained also in England and Scotland. In *The Winter's Tale* we hear of a Puritan who 'sings psalms to hornpipes', and popular songs such as 'Goe from my Window' are to be found in that remarkable publication entitled *Ane Compendious Book of Godly and Spirituall Sangis Collectit out of Sundry parts of the Scripture with sundry other Ballats changet out of prophaine sangis for avoyding of sin and harlatry, with augmentation of sundrye gude and godly Ballates*, etc., etc., printed in Edinburgh in 1567.[9]

The practice of borrowing folk tunes for religious purposes has never ceased. In Wales in the mid-eighteenth century the airs adopted for congregational hymn-singing in the Nonconformist churches were largely folk tunes;[10] and in more recent times the *English Hymnal* and other hymn-collections contain many folk tunes which the compilers have set to religious poems. An old singer once

---

[8] See Franz M. Böhme, *Altdeutsches Liederbuch* (Leipzig, 1913, 2nd ed.).

[9] See article by Anne G. Gilchrist in *Journal of the English Folk Dance Society*, iii (1938), no. 3, p. 157.

[10] See W. S. Gwynn Williams, *Welsh National Music and Dance*, p. 73 (London, 1932).

said to the Reverend S. Baring-Gould: 'If I go to chapel, I hear funny songs there. The words be good enough, but the tunes—hang me, when I hear them I want to put the old words to 'em.' And then he added: 'But they always ties up the tails of these tunes in a fashion I don't like.' Probably he was expressing disapproval of the regularizing of the tunes he had known in a freer state.

Folk tunes were introduced as *canti fermi* into secular as well as religious motets and, as domestic music developed, folk airs were used side by side with composed melodies in part-songs and madrigals and also in instrumental music. Our English collections of virginal music are particularly rich in arrangements of folk tunes, e.g. 'John come kiss me now', 'The woods so wild', and 'Sellenger's Round'. Of course, the use of a folk tune in a composition usually means adaptation as well as adoption, and as we have no means of comparing these tunes with their contemporary forms we cannot always say with certainty if they are pure folk tunes or not.

During the eighteenth century, the ballad opera became a favourite form of entertainment. The lyrics, which alternated with spoken dialogue, were set mainly to adaptations of existing airs, and many of them were derived from folk songs. The most popular of the ballad operas in England was *The Beggar's Opera* (1728) by John Gay, with music arranged by John Pepusch. It was preceded three years earlier by *The Gentle Shepherd* by Allan Ramsay in which the tunes were taken from Scottish sources.

The popular tunes of the town have always to some extent percolated into the country, where they have found a home side by side with the traditional airs or become translated into the folk idiom. A good example of the way in which the folk will transform a tune is to be seen in the following versions of 'The Maid of the Mill'. The first is from William Shield's opera *Rosina* (1783); the second is the tune that the fiddler of the Morris dancers plays every Whit Monday at

Bampton in Oxfordshire; and the third is a mixolydian version noted from a fiddler in Bould, another Oxfordshire village. (Of course, it is just possible that Shield's tune was adapted from a folk tune.)

Ex. 5a

From William Shield's opera *Rosina* (1783)

Ex. 5b

Ex. 5c

In our own day we can say that the recent renascence of English art music is in part due to the influence of folk music.[11] In England, as in many European countries, notably Hungary, folk music has laid the basis of a national style of music and has freed the composer from the dominance of the musical idiom of Germany. This is nowhere more apparent than in the works of Vaughan Williams. He made many beautiful arrangements of folk songs and introduced folk themes into his own compositions, but the most important and far-reaching consequence of his contact with folk music was that it supplied him with a native idiom in which to express his own musical thoughts. The same is true of Gustav Holst, though he was not involved with folk music to the same extent as Vaughan Williams. There are other composers who have been directly affected by folk music, such as George Butterworth, to whom we shall refer later, and yet again there are others who have not gone directly to folk music for inspiration, but who have nevertheless been indirectly affected by it, in that they are speaking in a language which it has enriched.

[11] See Vaughan Williams, *National Music*, Ch. V.

3
Some Musical Characteristics

Because of the manner of its creation, described in Chapter 1, folk song has acquired certain fundamental characteristics. It is impersonal, because it is the expression of the community and not merely of the individual. It is sincere, because it has been evolved unconsciously: it exists for itself and not for some ulterior motive, such as to impress an audience. It is ageless, because, while its roots go back into the distant past, it is continuously bearing fresh blooms.

We should add that it is the expression of the nation, but this statement requires some qualification. Every country is to some extent influenced by the culture of other countries. Given time and the right conditions, alien elements will become absorbed and form part of the national tradition. We see it in language—particularly in our own language, which is compounded of many different elements. In our folk music we often come across themes which we are tempted to think of as typically English until we discover that they exist in the folk music of other countries. We then ask ourselves: which came first, or have they evolved independently?—a question we cannot always answer.

In considering nationality in folk music, we meet with the paradox that often what seems to be the most national is the most universal. This is easy to understand because the folk music of any people is that people's way of expressing the emotions and experiences that are common to mankind.

Professor Walter Wiora[1] gives many examples of connections or similarities between the folk tunes of various countries. He writes: 'What we meet everywhere are typical melodic and other *forms*, while the various nations' indi-

[1] See *European Folk Song* (Oxford University Press, 1966).

vidualities are expressed more in coloration and modification of these basic forms, rather than in the forms themselves.' He adds: 'Some nations are drawn more to certain such forms than to others, filling them, completing them, and changing them and giving them the stamp of their own styles and personalities, which again are expressions of their characters as nations.'

Folk music, as we have said, is not art-less music, though for the sake of convenience we have spoken of folk music and art music as though they were antithetic. Folk music, though it is the product of untutored artists, is not without art nor without science. Neither is folk music embryonic art, that is, music which is in the process of becoming art music. A good folk song (they are not, of course, all good) is complete in itself, just as a quartet of Haydn is complete in itself and not merely embryonic Beethoven.

Folk music has limits, but within these limits it fulfils the requirements of great art, which, as Vaughan Williams has said, are 'unity, variety, symmetry, development, and continuity'. Or, as a folk fiddler once said to me: 'I like music that's smooth, that counts out well, and has a pretty tune.'

Folk music is normally limited in the following respects:

(1) It is applied and not absolute music, i.e. it is designed as an integral part of song or dance and not as an end in itself.

(2) It is strophic, i.e. the same tune is repeated for the various stanzas of the song or the figures of the dance.

(3) Folk music (at least that of England and many other countries) is monodic.

These limits do not imply incompleteness, or restrict the range of artistic expression. They are the conditions which determine the form that the artistic expression shall take. We will consider briefly the manner in which they operate.

(1) *The relation of tune and words*. The folk musician would

agree with Plato that it is difficult to recognize the meaning of rhythm and melody when they are divorced from words or are not subordinated to the dance. To the folk singer the tune is a particularly effective way of telling a story and the words are usually uppermost in his mind. Many traditional singers in England are unable to sing a tune without the words. A Breton proverb runs: 'Celui qui perd ses mots perd son air.' Or, as an Essex folk singer said to Vaughan Williams: 'If you can get the words, the Almighty will send the tune.'

Text and tune are, however, by no means always inter-dependent. Cecil Sharp and others have come across instances in which singers who had 'lost their words' could still supply the tune. In the Appalachian Mountains of North America the singers were more tune-conscious than in England and Alexander Keith reports the same of the folk singers of Aberdeenshire.[2]

Then there are many instances in which a tune is transferred from one song to another. In certain cases, for instance that of 'Lord Lovel', the same tune (with variants) always accompanies the ballad, while in others the ballad or song is accompanied by a variety of different tunes. Such is 'The Cruel Mother', which incidentally always seems to attract a beautiful tune. The reason for this divergence of practice is a matter for speculation.[3]

This leads us to consider the question of 'tune families', which may have some bearing on the interchangeability of tunes. The subject has been fully discussed by Samuel P. Bayard.[4] He describes a tune family as 'a group of melodies

[2] See *Last Leaves of Traditional Ballads*, p. xlii (Aberdeen, 1925).

[3] Various suggestions are put forward by B. H. Bronson in his article 'The Interdependence of Ballad Tunes and Texts' in *The Ballad as Song* (also included in *The Critics and the Ballad*), edited MacEdward Leach and Tristram P. Coffin (Southern Illinois University Press, 1961).

[4] See 'Prolegomena to a Study of the Principal Melodic Families of Folk Song', in Ch. 8 of *The Critics and the Ballad*; also Bronson, 'The Interdependence of Ballad Tunes and Texts' and 'Samuel Hall's Family Tree' (Ch. 2 of *The Ballad as Song*).

showing basic interrelation by means of constant melodic correspondence, and presumably owing their mutual likeness to descent from a single air that has assumed multiple forms through processes of variation, imitation and assimilation'. He believes that further examination of the tunes would reveal resemblances between them pointing to the existence of a more limited number of tune families than would be suspected from a first glance.

The association between language and tune shows itself in many directions. In the funeral laments of Central and Eastern Europe the transition from speech to song is sometimes almost imperceptible. Vaughan Williams[5] describes song as nothing less than 'speech charged with emotion'. He gives as illustration the exhortation of an open-air preacher who, as he warmed to his subject, gradually made use of certain definite notes in the inflection of his voice until the following musical theme emerged:

This might be called the raw material of song and in fact we find that this theme forms the basis of a number of phrases in English folk song. In a slightly more developed form it appears as the opening phrase of 'Searching for Lambs', one of the most beautiful of all folk songs, and in many other tunes.

Ex. 6

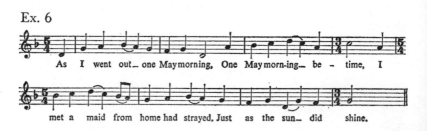

As I went out— one May morning, One May morn-ing— be - time, I met a maid from home had strayed. Just as the sun— did shine.

5 *National Music* pp. 31 ff.

What makes you rise so soon, my dear,
Your journey to pursue?
Your pretty little feet they tread so sweet,
Strike off the morning dew.

I'm going to feed my father's flock,
His young and tender lambs,
That over hills and over dales
Lie waiting for their dams.

O stay! O stay! you handsome maid,
And rest a moment here,
For there is none but you alone
That I do love so dear.

How gloriously the sun doth shine,
How pleasant is the air;
I'd rather rest on a true love's breast
Than any other where.

For I am thine and thou art mine;
No man shall uncomfort thee.
We'll join our hands in wedded bands
And a-married we will be.

Stock phrases, or commonplaces, such as this are, as it were, the framework upon which the traditional singer weaves his pattern of song, though it would be misleading to suggest that they all arose from a musical stylization of natural speech inflection. They are perhaps most obvious at the beginning of the tune, forming a sort of musical 'As I walked out'. A favourite opening is that of a descending passage from dominant to tonic, as is also an ascending passage from tonic to dominant. Those who are interested will be able to discover for themselves many other stock phrases from an examination of the tunes in the various folk song collections. Several further examples are given in *English Folk Song: Some Conclusions*.

The close association of language and tune is to be seen in matters of rhythm as well as in melodic outline, for instance in the frequent occurrence of the anacrusis at the beginning of the phrase and in the small number of feminine endings at the conclusion of the phrase. When these feminine endings do occur in the text the accompanying musical cadence is often very beautiful and expressive, as in 'Barbara Ellen'.

Ex. 7

However, feminine endings seem occasionally to be avoided by laying the stress on the second syllable of a word instead of the first, for instance, 'gar-dén', 'coun-tríe', 'cas-tél' (castle).

(2) *Some features of the melodic stanza*. The number of phrases that make up a musical stanza, the way in which they are combined, their number, metre, compass, and shape, all vary. The four-line phrase is the most usual, and ABCD (i.e. four different phrases) is the most common form, but many other combinations, such as ABBA, AABA, and ABAC, are to be found. The ABBA form, with the A phrase ending on the tonic, usually twice repeated in the final bar, and the B phrase ending on the dominant, is commonly

used for the 'Come all ye' type of song. It is sometimes
thought that its English use may have been derived from
Ireland, though the fact that the form is but rarely used in
Gaelic songs would seem to be against this. Furthermore,
this kind of structure is to be found in other European
countries. Cecil Sharp's reference to it as the stock-in-trade
of the English folk singer is apt, for he uses it frequently and
will often have recourse to a tune of this pattern when he
cannot remember the tune that habitually accompanies
the song. Melodies cast in this form tend to become stereotyped, though some inventiveness is often displayed by
varying the repetition of the B phrase, as in this example of
'The Banks of the Sweet Dundee'.

Ex. 8

In many songs, and particularly in ballads, the refrain is
a characteristic feature, but we shall be speaking of this
later.

The most common form of metre is composed of alternate
lines of four and three stresses, known as ballad or common
metre, but long metre, four lines of four feet, is also prevalent. This reminds us of the passage in *A Midsummer
Night's Dream* when Quince proposes that the prologue to
'Pyramus and Thisbe' shall be written in eight and six.
'No, make it two more,' says Bottom. 'Let it be written in
eight and eight.'

Iambic and dactylic verse are both in common use, but there are many hybrids. As in early English alliterative poetry, and the 'new principle' on which Coleridge constructed his *Christabel*, there is constant irregularity in the number of syllables contained in the corresponding lines of the successive stanzas of the text without a change in the number of stresses. This involves variations in the splitting up of time values, which the folk singer achieves with great skill.

A frequent rhythmic feature, by no means peculiar to English folk song, is the use of 5/4 time (2+3). In these tunes, the final bar of the second phrase often loses one or two beats, as in 'Barbara Ellen' (above) and 'Searching for Lambs' (p. 22). There are many other such irregularities in the folk songs of England, as well as those of other countries, but they are more apparent to the eye than to the ear, when the flow of the melody is not held up by the mechanical device of bar-lines. Thomas Moore, writing in 1807 to Stevenson (who made the accompaniments of Moore's 'Irish Melodies'), complains of the difficulty he is experiencing in the composition of his poems to Irish melodies because of the 'irregular structure of many of those airs and the lawless kind of metre to which it will in consequence be necessary to adapt them'.[6]

There is considerable variety of compass in English folk song. There are tunes with a small compass, such as 'The Keys of Canterbury' which is restricted to a range of five notes (with the addition of an auxiliary note).

[6] *Journal of the Irish Folk Song Society*, xlv, p. 12.

Ex. 9

On the other hand, many tunes cover a wide compass. In these the rise of an octave is a favourite interval, as in 'My Bonny Boy' (p. 28) and 'The Seeds of Love' (p. 93), while sometimes an interval as great as a tenth will occur:

Ex. 10

Some tunes are composed of short reiterated phrases as in 'The Keys of Canterbury' (Example 9), while others are made up of long, sweeping phrases, as in the tune quoted above.

The English folk singer seldom indulges in melisma. This beautiful tune is one of the exceptions:

Ex. 11

My Bonny Boy

Now once I was court-ed by a bor-ny, bon-ny boy,— I
loved him I vow and pro-test; I loved him so—
well, so ve-ry, ve-ry well, That I built him a—
bower in my breast,—   That I
built him a— bower in my breast.

On the contrary, he will sometimes go out of his way to provide a syllable for each note, resulting in the manufacture of such words as 'wor-del-kin' and 'tor-del-kin' (walking and talking) and 'prim-e-roses'. This seems in particular to be a habit of gypsy singers.

Ornaments, such as shakes, mordents, appoggiaturas, and slides, vary from singer to singer, but they are invariably so deftly introduced that they enrich without disturbing the melodic line. Irish folk singers are, as a rule, particularly lavish as regards ornamentation.

(3) *Monody.* English folk song is conceived as pure melody without accompanying harmony, either instrumental or vocal. The habit of singing with instrumental accompaniment is a modern innovation. In fact, some older traditional singers have been known to fail to recognize a tune played with an accompaniment. The point of view of the traditional singer was put to me by a Dorset singer in criticism of a B.B.C. concert singer's interpretation of a folk song. 'It's all too smoothed out,' he said, 'and the piano does spoil the

song.' And then he added: 'I suppose it's very nice for the singer to have a piano, but it does make it very awkward for the listeners.'

The absence of harmony has its compensations, for what the tune loses in harmonic texture it gains in melodic freedom. One instance of this is in the variety of modes that are used in English folk music. We shall be returning to this later.

One of the wonders of a good folk tune is that although it is repeated over and over again in the successive stanzas of the song and has no instrumental accompaniment to give variety, it seldom palls or ceases to provide an effective vehicle for the changing sentiments and situations of the text. This is particularly remarkable in narrative songs and ballads.

This is perhaps the place to say something of the traditional singer's style and technique of singing, which have evolved side by side with the song and are part of his inherited tradition. The folk singer might be said to carry out the injunction of Caccini, the sixteenth-century Florentine musician: 'Let music be first of all language and rhythm and secondly tone'—an echo of Plato's words. To the folk singer, the story he is telling or the experience he is relating is all-important, and the role of the tune is primarily to enhance and add significance to his utterance. A good folk singer is a past master of the welding together of words and tune. He manages to maintain the vocal line while enunciating his words clearly and giving to each its due proportion and emphasis. He follows the rule, so cogently stressed by Plunket Greene,[7] that you must sing as you speak. Not having learned the tune from the printed page, he is not tempted to give to each note its exact time value, but he will make almost imperceptible variations in order to accommodate the sense and rhythm of the words. Despite this

[7] *Interpretation in Song* (London, 1911).

flexibility of note-values the singer never loses the pulse of the music, and from the first note to the last it is a continuous whole. 'Sing through your rests,' says Plunket Greene. 'Remember it's what lies between the notes that makes the music,' said a folk fiddler.

There is a certain deliberateness in the singer's performance. He does not slur his words, and as well as articulating them clearly he has a fine sense of their colour. As a singer once described her mother's singing, 'Her tongue wrapped so lovingly round the words.'

We have already spoken of the habit of ornamentation and variation in the tune, which is practised by many singers. On the other hand, there is little variety in dynamics or change of tempo. The traditional singer feels no need to make points, but is content to act as the medium through which the plain unvarnished tale is told. He will often close his eyes while singing or seem to fix his gaze on some far-distant object. At the end of the song he will usually repeat the last line in a speaking voice, as though he needed a period of transition before returning to the everyday world.

The repertory of the English traditional singer is not, of course, limited to folk songs. He will sing other types of songs freely and will make no distinction between folk songs and other 'old songs' that he may have heard from an older generation. In fact, the term 'folk song' would have been unknown to him before the days of the revival. Yet his style in the performance of folk songs will often differ subtly from that adopted in other songs.

4
The Modes

In this chapter I shall not attempt to give an historical or scientific account of the modes, but I shall limit myself to a short description of those that are commonly used in English folk tunes.[1]

For all practical purposes we can say that English folk tunes are cast in the heptatonic (7-note) diatonic scale, i.e. alternating series of intervals of two and three whole-tones, respectively, with an interval of a semitone between the two series. Any seven consecutive white notes of the piano will form a diatonic scale. Taking each of the white notes in turn as the tonic we get the possibility of seven different modes, as shown below.

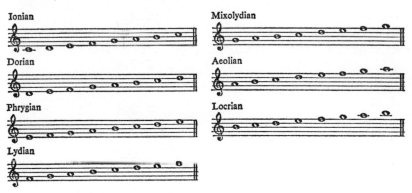

These modes should not, however, be thought of as a series of ascending or descending notes. It is the relationship of the notes to the tonic, the key-note, that is important. Though for convenience sake the modes have been given as

[1] For a fuller account, see Sharp, *English Folk Song: Some Conclusions*, Ch. v; B. H. Bronson, 'Folk Song and the Modes', in *The Ballad as Song*, p. 79 (Berkeley, 1969); and the many musical dictionaries.

though on the white notes of the piano, they must not be thought of as segments of the scale of C major starting on different notes of the scale, nor must they be confused with pitch. Each of the modes can start at any pitch and the key-signature will vary accordingly.

The Greek-derived names by which these modes are distinguished are not in accordance with ancient Greek practice, but were applied at a later date and are those used at the present time, at any rate in England. The Locrian mode, dubbed by the church a 'bastard' mode owing to the discordant relationship between B and F (taking B as the tonic), is not used in English folk music and so need not be considered. The Lydian and Phrygian modes occur but rarely; so this leaves us with four modes, the Ionian, Mixolydian, Dorian, and Aeolian, which are in general use. For the sake of convenience we will reduce them to a common key.

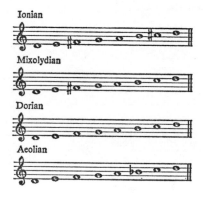

It will be seen that two of the modes have a major third and two have a minor third. Of the two with the major third, the Ionian corresponds to the major scale; and the Mixolydian mode differs from it only in the seventh degree of the scale which is flattened. Of the minor modes, or rather those with a minor third, the Aeolian is the same as the descending melodic minor (a harmonic minor scale is practically unknown in English folk music); and the Dorian differs from the Aeolian in that the sixth degree is not flattened.

There is an additional form of classification, which is according to the relation of the range to the tonic. Scales lying between the tonic and its octave are called 'authentic', whereas scales between the dominant and its octave are called 'plagal' and the term 'hypo' is affixed to the mode in question. Cecil Sharp considered the distinction to be of little importance, but others, among them Professor Bronson, believe that 'the range has a significant relation to the shape of the tune'.[2]

The modes are not only of scientific interest. The character, colour, and shape of a melody are affected by the particular mode in which it is cast.

A number of tunes in the Aeolian mode are given in this book, e.g. 'The Cuckoo', 'The Duke of Bedford', 'As I Walked Out', 'My Bonny Boy', 'The Coasts of High Barbary', 'Down in Yon Forest', and 'Bushes and Briars'. Below are two versions of 'The Gypsy Laddie', one in the Aeolian and the other in the Mixolydian mode:

Ex. 12a

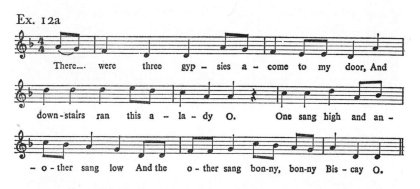

There... were three gyp - sies a - come to my door, And down-stairs ran this a - la - dy O. One sang high and an - o - ther sang low And the o - ther sang bon-ny, bon-ny Bis - cay O.

[2] See *The Traditional Tunes of the Child Ballads*, i, p. xxviii.

Ex. 12b

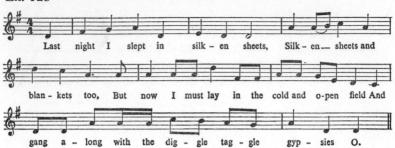

And two versions of 'Henry Martin', of which the first is in the Mixolydian and the second in the Dorian mode:

Ex. 13a

Ex. 13b

The frequency of this or that mode will vary with the individual singer, but taken as a whole there is a considerable preponderance of tunes in the Ionian mode. This is probably due to a great extent to the influence of the major scale, but it would be a mistake to regard the Ionian mode as being necessarily more modern than the other modes. It has always been a favourite with the folk and for that reason was called *modus lascivus* in the Middle Ages and excluded from the Divine Office. Zarlino, the sixteenth-century Venetian musician and theorist, observed that peasants without any art proceed by the interval of the semitone in forming their closes. But though the Ionian mode corresponds to the major scale as regards its notes, there is a subtle distinction in that the notes are not employed to make harmonic progressions.

A few words should be said about the pentatonic scales. A pentatonic scale, as its name implies, is a 5-note scale. In the form in which it is most familiar to Western ears it possesses no semitones, the intervals between the notes consisting of whole-tones and one-and-a-half tones (minor thirds).

Tunes in the pentatonic modes are often referred to as 'gapped', but this is misleading because it implies that the tune is incomplete, which is not the case. A tune in a 5-note scale is no less complete than one in a 7-note scale, any more than a quartet is less complete than a septet or a symphony. The following pentatonic tune, for instance, shows no sign of incompleteness:

Ex. 14

The Nightingale

One— morn-ing, one— morn-ing, one— morn-ing in— May I saw— a fair cou-ple a – – mak-ing their way; O one was a la-dy, so bright and so— fair, And the o – ther was a sol – dier, a— brave vol - un - teer.

Again for convenience we will exemplify the pentatonic modes by taking the white notes of the piano, but eliminating E and B. (The black notes can also serve as an illustration.) According to the relative position of the tonic, there are five pentatonic modes, i.e.

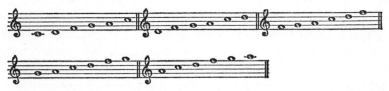

The tonic of a pentatonic scale is, however, not so well defined as that of a heptatonic scale. For that reason some scholars tend not to differentiate between the modes of a pentatonic scale but to regard them as segments of the same scale.

There are but few instances of a pure pentatonic tune among those recovered in England, though they are prevalent in the folk songs of the Appalachian Mountains and to a certain extent in other parts of America; and they are frequently found in Scotland in the folk music of the Lowlands and more particularly in the Gaelic music of the Highlands.

Whether or not the heptatonic scale is a development of the pentatonic is a question on which opinion is divided. Cecil Sharp's view was that the heptatonic scale is an extension of the pentatonic in which the 'missing' notes are filled in by one of the combinations E♭ and B♭, E♮ and B♮, or E♮ and B♭. In the transition from the pentatonic scale the medial notes are introduced with some uncertainty. They may be used as auxiliary or passing notes, or they may be indeterminate in pitch. Sometimes the notes vary from major to minor in the same tune: a device which is often very expressive. In English folk tunes, the third, sixth, and seventh are often so affected. In the following example the third and seventh are inflected.

Ex. 15

As I Walked through the Meadows

As I walk'd through 'the mea-dows to take— the fresh air, The— flow-ers were bloom-ing and gay, I— heard a —young dam-sel so sweet-ly a-sing; Her— cheeks like the blos-som in May.

Though the pentatonic scale is rare in English folk music, there are a number of examples of hexatonic (6-note) scales in which the third, sixth, or seventh (usually the sixth) degree of the scale is missing. Examples of tunes without the sixth are 'Searching for Lambs' (p. 22) and 'The Seeds of Love' (p. 93).

Folk tunes rarely, if ever, modulate in the sense of a change of tonal centre, but the inflection of certain notes in a tune may be regarded as a change of mode.

As we have already said, not every folk tune will fit into a neat system of tabulation. There will always be exceptions and irregularities, not to mention tunes in which the tonic is doubtful, but the foregoing observations are applicable to the bulk of English folk music.

5

Ballads

Of all the various types of folk song the ballad[1] must take pride of place. The term 'ballad' is very loosely used in common parlance, but we are concerned here only with the traditional ballad. In this sense the ballad may be defined as 'a narrative song in which the action is focused on a single episode'.

The classic collection of ballads is Francis J. Child's *English and Scottish Popular Ballads* (1882–98). It contains 305 ballads, mostly with more than one version, notes on the ballads, and comparison with their foreign analogues. Most of the narratives that form the subject of the ballads are of Indo-European stock. Nearly all the ballads in the Child collection are from manuscript or printed sources. Child made several attempts to secure ballads that were still in oral tradition, but with little success. In 1873 he inserted a note in *Notes and Queries* appealing, in addition to manuscripts, for anything in the way of traditional ballads or fragments that yet remained in the memories of the people. And, writing next year to Svend Grundtvig, the great Danish scholar and editor of *Danmarks gamle Folkeviser*,[2] the classic collection of Danish ballads, he says:

The circular . . . which I sent to every clergyman and schoolmaster in Scotland (or to nearly 2,500 of them) produced almost *nothing*. I received a few copies of the better ballads, half-a-dozen from one place

[1] For further information, see G. H. Gerould, *The Ballad of Tradition*; E. K. Wells, *The Ballad Tree*; and M. J. C. Hodgart, *The Ballads* (London, 1950).

[2] Sven Grundtvig, Axel Olrik, H. Grüner Nielson *et al.*, *Danmarks Gamle Folkeviser* (10 vols., Copenhagen, 1853–1965). Reprint with additional English prefaces (1966–7). Vol. xi, music, in preparation.

or another, but I fear all of them are recollections of *modern print*, a most undesirable aftergrowth of oral tradition.[3]

He adds with truth that something more than a printed appeal is necessary. Had he had a detachment of field-collectors at his disposal, how different the story might have been!

The accompanying tunes are not included in Child's collection, except for fifty-five which appear in the Appendix. References are given to some published airs. These, according to Bronson, are written in another hand. Happily, Child's omission of the tunes has been more than made good by B. H. Bronson in his *Traditional Tunes of the Child Ballads with their Texts, according to the Extant Records of Great Britain and America* (4 vols., 1959–72). This monumental work contains 254 separate ballads with a total of over 4,000 tune variants. In addition there are comprehensive notes on the ballads and an analysis of the tunes. This work and the original Child collection form together a ballad literature which is unsurpassed.

The inclusion of certain ballads in the Child canon and the exclusion of others has sometimes been questioned. Unfortunately Child did not live to write an introduction to his great work informing us on what principles he had determined his selection. He wrote to Professor Grundtvig in August 1872: 'We cannot of course exclude all ballads which have not been taken from the mouths of the people —nor perhaps include all such,'[4] which indicates that he attached some weight to the factor of oral transmission.

Ballad style has been well described by William Motherwell who writes in his *Minstrelsy* (p. xli):

The action of the piece commences at once. . . . The story runs in an arrowlike stream, with all the straightforwardness of unfeigned and earnest passion. There is no turning back . . . to render more clear

---

[3] Quoted by S. B. Hustvedt, *Ballad Books and Ballad Men*, p. 263 (Harvard University Press, Cambridge, Mass., 1930).

[4] Quoted by Hustvedt, p. 253.

that which may have been dimly expressed and slightly hinted: and there is no pause made to gather on the way beautiful images or appropriate illustrations.

The absence of preliminary explanations and descriptions is a marked feature of the ballad, and the oft-quoted dictum of the poet Gray that 'it begins in the fifth act of the play' is apt. There is throughout economy of language and commonplaces take the place of particularized description. A ring is always 'gay gold', a comb is 'ivory', a horse is a 'milk-white steed', the heroine has 'long yellow locks', her hands are 'lily-white', and so on. The tragedy of the unfortunate lovers who lose their lives and are buried side by side usually ends with some such lines:

> And out of his grave there grew a red rose
> And out of hers a briar.
> They twisted and twined in a true love's knot
> For all true loves to admire.

> or

> And the rose wrapped round the briar.

The commonplaces or stock phrases serve as landmarks which help the memory of the singer. And instead of creating monotony, as one might expect, they tend to free the imagination.

Occasionally there will be a reference to some small detail, as in King Lear's 'Pray you, undo this button', which lightens up the whole scene and enhances the sense of tragedy. For instance, when the little foot-page sets out on his errand, how better could the feeling of urgency be expressed than by the lines:

> And he being in haste to carry the news,
> He buckled his shoes as he ran.

One of the outstanding techniques sometimes employed in the unfolding of a ballad story is the repetition of a theme with slight variations, thereby creating a feeling of tension, and gradually leading to the denouement. This is what is called 'incremental repetition', a phrase that was brought into prominence by F. B. Gummere.[5] A typical example is:

Ex. 16

Lord Rendal

Where have you been all the day, Ren - dal, my son?
Where have you been all the day my pret - ty one? I've
been to my sweet-heart, mo - ther, I've been to my sweet-heart,
L'istesso tempo
mo - ther, — Make my bed soon, For I'm
sick at my heart and I fain would lie down.

What have you been eating, Rendal, my son?
What have you been eating, my pretty one?
O eels and eel broth, mother, O eels and eel broth, mother.
Make my bed soon, for I'm sick to my heart and I fain would lie down.

Where did she get them from, Rendal, my son?
Where did she get them from, my pretty one?
From hedges and ditches, mother, from hedges and ditches, mother.
Make my bed soon, for I'm sick to my heart and I fain would lie down.

What was the colour on their skin, Rendal, my son?
What was the colour on their skin, my pretty one?
O spickit and sparkit, mother, O spickit and sparkit, mother.
Make my bed soon, for I'm sick to my heart and I fain would lie down.

What will you leave your father, Rendal, my son?
What will you leave your father, my pretty one?
My lands and houses, mother, my lands and houses, mother.
Make my bed soon, for I'm sick to my heart and I fain would lie down.

[5] See *The Popular Ballad* (Boston, 1967).

What will you leave your mother, etc.
My gold and silver, etc.

What will you leave your brother, etc.
My cows and horses, etc.

What will you leave your lover, etc.
A rope to hang her, etc.

Another rhetorical device is a kind of parallelism in which an action is described in phrases akin to those that have previously been used by one of the characters in speech, as, for instance, in these stanzas from 'Little Musgrave' (or Matthy Groves, as he is popularly called).

You may strike the very first lick,
You must strike it like a man;
And I will strike the very next lick
I'll kill you if I can.

Little Matthy struck the very first lick,
He wounded deep and sore;
Lord Darnel struck the very next lick.
Little Matthy struck no more.

Similarly a question will be answered in nearly the same words as it is asked.

The refrain often forms an important element in ballad structure. It may be external, occurring at the end of the stanza or, more usually, internal, being interspersed between the narrative lines. The refrain occurs also in the song, but less frequently than in the ballad. Sometimes it consists of words that have a connection with the ballad or song, as in the following:

Ex. 17

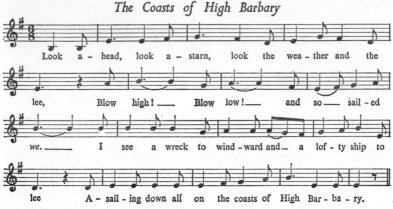

The Coasts of High Barbary

Look a - head, look a - starn, look the wea - ther and the lee, Blow high! __ Blow low! __ and so __ sail - ed we. __ I see a wreck to wind - ward and __ a lof - ty ship to lee A - sail - ing down all on the coasts of High Bar - ba - ry.

At other times it has no connection, but appears to consist of words arbitrarily introduced, such as

Ex. 18

Scarborough Fair

Where are˙ you go - ing?˙ To Scar-borough Fair? Par - sley, sage, - rose - - ma - ry and thyme, Re - mem-ber me to a bon - ny lass there, __ For once __ she was a true lo - ver of mine.

Again, at other times the refrain has developed into a jingle of meaningless syllables, e.g. 'rue dum day fol the diddle dol' and 'To my oor bag boor bag nigger bag waller and bantabaloo'. (For an interesting account of refrains with meaningless syllables in Gaelic waulking songs, see J. L. Campbell and Francis Collinson: *Hebridean Folk Songs* (Oxford, 1969).) Some have seen in this jingling refrain the corruption of ancient ritual words, but it is impossible to prove whether or not this is so.

Paradoxically, these meaningless syllables seem to repre-

sent the quintessence of a national language. Cecil Sharp
has related that when he was coaching Yvette Guilbert,
the French *diseuse*, in English folk song she found the
pronunciation of these syllables harder to master than anything else in the song.

Little is known of the age of the ballads. The earliest
recorded ballad is that of 'Judas' (Child 23) which appears
in a manuscript of the late thirteenth century, but may have
existed at an earlier date. As a matter of fact, E. K. Chambers
questions whether 'Judas' should be regarded as a popular
ballad and believes it to be of ecclesiastical origin. He considers that the first really popular ballads in Child's collection are 'Robin Hood and the Monk' (119) and 'Riddles
Wisely Expounded' (1), both found in manuscripts of
about 1450.[6] It has been conjectured that a number of
ballads date from the fifteenth or sixteenth century, but that
the ballad form may be considerably older. There is, however, but scanty evidence. According to G. L. Kittredge
there are only eleven ballads extant in manuscript older
than the seventeenth century.[7]

On the 'Golden Age' of balladry there has been much
speculation. In this connection we cannot do better than to
quote the convincing words of Professor Bronson:

Apart from the Robin Hood cycle, it is untrue, though it has been
carelessly said, that the best ballads, in the sense of the most artistically
satisfying, are the oldest. It is one thing to say that the best ballads are
the oldest ones, and another to say that the best ballad texts are variants
of ballads known to be very old. But I suspect the distinction has
seldom been borne in mind. . . . The best ballad, aesthetically, is the
most beautiful variant, not an infelicitous ancestor of such a variant.
And, generally speaking, the best texts in Child's great collection date
from near the close of the eighteenth century.[8]

[6] *English Literature at the Close of the Middle Ages*, p. 183 (Oxford, 1945).
[7] *English and Scottish Popular Ballads*, edited from the collection of Francis
James Child (Boston, 1905).
[8] *The Ballad as Song*, p. 104 (University of California Press, 1969).

He adds that it may well be that the fifteenth century was a Golden Age of balladry, as has often been declared, 'for conditions so far as we can tell were favourable', but that 'looking at the extant record, we must certainly agree that the *eighteenth* century was *a* Golden Age of balladry'.

This leads us to consider the origin of the ballads. Apart from the fact that they have been moulded by oral transmission we know very little. There has been heated and at times acrid controversy on the subject for many generations.

To sum up quite shortly, the two extreme opinions are (1) that the ballads were composed by the minstrels, the earliest professional musicians; and (2) that they arose as a spontaneous utterance of the community in association with the dance.[9]

As regards the first theory, we have to bear in mind that there have been various types of minstrels. There were those who were attached to the higher order of society and were often themselves of noble blood, and there were the wandering entertainers who catered for the common people. Gerould writes:

There is no reason why such minstrels as were not hangers-on of great houses but entertained the squire, the townsman, and the lower orders of country folk, should not have made ballads according to the popular mode, and have added them to their repertories. Even though what the minstrel composed might in the first state be somewhat more conscious than ballads otherwise fashioned, and might lack certain qualities that we regard as characteristic, it would soon be reformed in popular transmission. Such professional vagabonds as I have in mind, moreover, would themselves have been so little differentiated from the people to whom they sang that they must have often been in the current of the tradition.[10]

[9] The chief exponent of this theory was Gummere. See *The Popular Ballad* (Boston, 1907).
[10] *The Ballad of Tradition*, pp. 225–6.

It is, in fact, reasonable to assume that minstrels, as well as other individuals, have played a part in the creation of ballads, but that subsequently their shape has been determined by the factor of communal *choice*, which is a very different thing from spontaneous communal *composition*.

The theory has sometimes been put forward that the ballad is derived from the epic. But again we would quote Gerould:

> The epic is admittedly the most ancient of literary *genres*, and the epic is something with a large canvas. The ballad, on the other hand, wherever we find it, is concentrated; the action is so massed that we do not get the effect of a skeletonized story, but of a unified short story, a story complete in itself. . . . Whatever be the truth about the way epics developed, the manner of presenting a tale in the ballad is different, and it has persisted through the centuries down to our own time.[11]

On the other hand, the epic may be to some extent a 'development—by elaboration and accretion—of the ballads themselves'.[12]

'A Gest of Robyn Hode' (Child 117), which has been called by Child 'a popular epic', is an example of the piecing together of several smaller ballads.

The word 'ballad' is derived from *ballare* (to dance), as in the word 'ballet', and it may originally have been applied to a dance-song, though to what extent the traditional ballad with which we are concerned was at one time associated with the dance is a moot point. Though it proves nothing, it is of interest that the name 'ballet' should still be given by folk singers to the written or printed copy of the words of a song.

In the Faroe Islands ballads sung to an accompaniment of the dance are still performed. In Britain, songs were on occasion doubtless accompanied by dance, but the custom

---

11 *The Ballad of Tradition*, p. 86.
12 See William Morris Hart, *Ballad and Epic : A Study in the Development of the Narrative Art* (Boston, 1907).

has long since died out and only survives in children's singing-games. There are many instances of dance-tunes being borrowed for songs and vice versa; for instance, in the *Complaynt of Scotland* (1549) a description is given of the recreation of a group of shepherds which includes story-telling, songs, and dances. The titles of three of the dances are given as 'Robin hude, Thom of lyn and Ihonne ermistrangie dance', which are evidently the well-known ballads, 'Robin Hood', 'Tam Lin', and 'Johnny Armstrong'. This does not mean, however, that they were sung and danced simultaneously.

Whether or not the ballads were formerly danced, the accompanying tunes are sometimes, if not actual dance-airs, tunes with a dance-like rhythm. This setting of a tragic text to a gay tune does not have the incongruous effect that one might imagine. On the contrary, it seems to heighten the tension. And one can understand the Clown in *The Winter's Tale*: 'I love a ballad even too well, if it be a doleful matter merrily set down.' Here is such a ballad, which is one of the most popular on both sides of the Atlantic.

Ex. 19

Lord Thomas and Fair Ellinor

Lord Tho-mas he was— a bold fo-res-ter And a
keep-er of the king's deer;— Fair El-li-nor she was a
la-dy gay,— Lord Tho-mas he loved— her dear.—

Now riddle my riddle, dear mother, said he,
And riddle it all in one;
Whether I shall marry the brown girl,
Or bring Fair Ellinor home.

The brown girl she has both houses and land,
Fair Ellinor she has none;
Wherefore I charge you upon my blessing
To bring the brown girl home.

He dressed himself all in his best,
His merry men all in white;
And every town that he passed through
They took him to be some knight.

He rode till he came to Fair Ellinor's bower,
He jingled so loud at the ring.
And who so ready as Fair Ellinor
To let Lord Thomas in.

What news, what news? Fair Ellinor cried,
What news have you brought to me?
I've come to ask you to my wedding.
Is that good news to thee?

Bad news, bad news, Lord Thomas, she said,
Bad news you bring to me.
I thought that I was to be the bride
And you the bridegroom to be.

Now riddle my riddle, dear mother, she said,
And riddle it all in one;
Whether I shall go to Lord Thomas's wedding,
Or tarry with you at home.

O hundreds are your friends, dear daughter,
And thousands are your foes;
Therefore I charge you upon my blessing,
To Lord Thomas's wedding don't go.

She dressed herself all in her best,
Her merry men all in green;
And every town that she rode through
They took her to be some queen.

She rode till she came to Lord Thomas's bower,
She jingled so loud at the ring.
And who so ready as Lord Thomas himself
To let Fair Ellinor in.

He took her by the lily-white hand
And led her across the hall.
There were four and twenty gay ladies,
But she was the fairest of all.

Is this your bride, Lord Thomas? she said.
I think she looks wonderful brown;
When you might have had as fair a young woman
As ever trod England's ground.

The brown girl had a penknife in her hand
It was both keen and sharp,
She put the handle in her hand
And pricked Fair Ellinor's heart.

O what is the matter? Lord Thomas he said.
What! can't you plainly see?
What! can't you see my own heart's blood
Come trickling down my knee?

Lord Thomas had a sword by his side,
It was both sharp and small.
He cut his bride's head right off her shoulders
And dashed it against the wall.

O dig me a grave, dear mother, he said,
And dig it both wide and deep;
And lay Fair Ellinor at my right side
And the brown girl at my feet.

Lord Thomas he put the sword in the ground,
The point at his own heart.
There were never three lovers that met together
That ever so quickly did part.

Note. The singer was unable to remember the beginning of the song, and the first nine stanzas have been taken from versions collected by Cecil Sharp.

The subject-matter of the ballads varies considerably. There are historical ballads, border-raid ballads, ballads of Robin Hood, and a few on religious, or semi-religious, subjects, but the majority, at any rate of those that have survived traditionally, are romantic ballads, mostly of a tragic nature.

Many ballads with supernatural elements which figure in the Child canon have disappeared from recent tradition, but some have survived, such as 'The Cruel Mother' (20) and 'The Wife of Usher's Well' (79) in which the babes or young children return from the grave to reproach their mothers, and there are also several in which the lover speaks from the grave to his betrothed.[13]

Embedded in the ballads are various elements of superstition and folk lore.[14]

[13] For a fuller account, see Wells, *The Ballad Tree*, Ch. 5.
[14] See L. C. Wimberley, *Folklore in the English and Scottish Ballads* (Chicago, 1928).

6
Categories of Folk Song

Folk songs can be divided into two main groups: (1) those that are not connected with any particular occasion; and (2) those that are associated with a certain season, ceremony, or function. For want of a better term we might call them non-functional and functional songs.

The first group can be divided roughly between the ballad (which was the subject of the preceding chapter) and other songs or lyrics. In discussing the ballad we have hitherto restricted the use of the term to the type of ballad included in the Child canon, which might be called the 'classical' ballad. There are, however, many other narrative songs to which the term could be applied. Indeed, it is almost impossible to draw a hard-and-fast dividing line between the ballad and other narrative songs. In Cecil Sharp's collection alone there are some thirty narrative songs not included in Child's collection which might be called ballads without doing violence to the term. Many of these ballads, such as 'The Three Butchers', and 'The Blind Beggar's Daughter of Bethnal Green', can be traced back several centuries. Others, particularly those that are associated with a particular event, are more recent, e.g. 'Maria Martin' which is based on a murder which took place in 1824.

In early collections, editors have not as a rule bothered overmuch about the distinction between 'ballad' and 'song'. When Bishop Percy was thinking of compiling his *Reliques* (see p. 72), the poet William Shenstone suggested to him the advisability of using the term 'ballad' **only** for a poem 'which describes or implies some action' and the **term** 'song' for one 'which contains only an expression of sentiment'.[1]

[1] See E. K. Chambers, *English Literature at the Close of the Middle Ages*, p. 143 (Clarendon Press, 1943).

Generally speaking, the songs or lyrics are rather more subjective than the ballads, though they still maintain their impersonal character. The 'I' of the folk song is not personified, but might relate to any man or woman. Another characteristic of the English folk song is the comparative absence of scenic description. 'The banks of sweet primroses' or the tree that 'spreads its branches around' are commonplaces which are used indiscriminately to set the scene for the action of the story.

The songs have many varied themes. The majority are concerned with the diverse aspects of love. Love and courtship, without any extraneous element, form perhaps the largest class, of which 'Searching for Lambs', quoted on p. 22, is one of the most beautiful examples.

The lover's farewell, or his absence and return, figure prominently, as does the tale of lovers who are thwarted by hard-hearted parents. The latter is a relic of the days when the consent of parents had to be obtained before marriage. There are, too, many tales of crafty and adventurous maidens who adopt various tricks to achieve their object, and the maid who puts on 'man's apparel' and follows her true love to sea is a favourite figure. As in real life, there are often 'false-hearted lovers', as well as tales of seduction.

Contrary to current opinion, there is very little that one could call indecent or bawdy in songs which are concerned with the relation of the sexes. In the early part of the century collectors found it necessary to omit from their publications a few forthright expressions which with the freer conventions of the present day would be accepted without question. Unfortunately the bringing to light of a few of these outspoken lines, hitherto unpublished, has led to a false impression of the original unedited words. In the true idiom of the people a delicate and often poetic symbolism is to be found which is far removed from the *double entendre* of more sophisticated members of society.

Folk song ranges over many subjects besides love. There

are songs about country life and occupations. These include the illegitimate pastime of poaching, but hunting songs are rare. Songs about sailors and the sea are popular and there are many that tell of fights at sea, including the exploits of pirates. There are no songs of the 'Home Sweet Home' type, nor patriotic songs such as 'Rule Britannia'. There are, however, songs about national heroes such as Nelson, Marlborough, and General Wolfe. These heroes are not confined to those of our own country, for Napoleon is a frequent figure. But the folk singer is perhaps even more interested in robbers, highwaymen, and rovers than in national heroes. On the lighter side, one gets a number of nonsense and nursery songs,[2] and a few humorous songs which are mainly concerned with the ineptitudes of wooers. Generally speaking, there is no differentiation between the tunes which accompany the ballads and those which accompany the songs.

Cumulative songs are known in all European countries and England is no exception. The cumulative song is one which grows progressively longer, each stanza consisting more or less of a repetition of the previous one but with added words. The well-known 'Twelve Days of Christmas' is such a song. Sometimes the song is repeated in reverse and becomes shorter as it progresses, arriving back as in the beginning. It is said that this type of song is sometimes used as a test for sobriety. There are also songs in which the stanzas are repeated with the change of a few words, but do not increase in length. An example is 'Dashing away with the Smoothing Iron' in which the successive days of the week and their appropriate occupations are named. Such songs are usually called enumerative songs.

Here we should say a few words about the industrial songs, which have only fairly recently been brought to

[2] The standard collection of nursery rhymes (without tunes) is *The Oxford Dictionary of Nursery Rhymes*, edited by Iona and Peter Opie (Clarendon Press, Oxford, 1951).

light, mainly through the efforts of A. L. Lloyd.[3] It is questionable whether these should be included under the category of folk songs, but they occupy a position on the periphery and some bear a marked influence of folk song. They are, to quote Mr. Lloyd, 'the kind of vernacular songs made by workers themselves directly out of their own interests and aspirations, and incidentally passed on among themselves mainly by oral means, though this is no *sine qua non*'.

From a sociological point of view the songs are interesting, but they seldom reach a high artistic level, as do so many of our folk songs, perhaps because they have not been subjected for a sufficiently long time to the moulding and refining influences of oral tradition. But on this point the reader should judge for himself by examining the songs.

A great deal of the folk character of the songs is due to the influence of Irish labourers who immigrated in large numbers in the middle of the nineteenth century. In this connection, Mr. Lloyd discusses the ABBA form, mentioned on pp. 24–5. He thinks it is probably of urban origin and he questions whether it is 'a conscious attempt at intensified artistry, or is merely a mark of decadence, of a slack following of the line of least resistance by repeating a phrase instead of inventing or memorizing a new one'. However that may be, 'the fact remains', writes Mr. Lloyd, 'that by the end of the eighteenth century it was well established in Irish song, and during the nineteenth century the form spread rapidly in rural and industrial areas throughout England. . . . In fact, it became the characteristic song-form for most traditions of late growth.' In the same category as the industrial songs in England we might place the songs that have arisen in homogeneous communities such as the cowboys and the lumberjacks of America.

We now come to what we have called the 'functional' songs: these may be divided into four groups, though more

[3] See *Folk Songs of England*, Ch. v, and *Come All Ye Bold Miners* (London, 1952).

are to be found in some other countries. These groups consist of:

(1) Carols.
(2) Work-songs (chanteys).
(3) Street-cries.
(4) Children's singing-games.

The term carol[4] embraces a fairly wide range. The definition given by the Reverend H. R. Bramley in Bramley and Stainer's *Christmas Carols* (1865) will serve as well as any: 'A kind of popular song appropriated to some special season of the ecclesiastical or natural year.'

Folk carols are distinct from ecclesiastical carols, though most of them have a religious orientation. The majority are associated with the Nativity or relate legends of the Gospel characters or the story of the Passion, while others are connected with the New Year or May Day. In the carol below, 'The Cherry Tree', the story is a variant of that related in Pseudo-Matthew, Chapter 1.

Ex. 20

Jo - seph was an old man, And an old man was he; And
Jo - seph mar-ried Ma - ry, The Queen of Ga - li - lee, And
Jo - seph mar-ried Ma - ry, The Queen of Ga - li - lee.

4 The standard work on the carol is R. L. Greene, *The Early English Carol*. (This deals with the medieval carol and only incidentally with the folk carol.) Other works on the carol in general are Erik Routley, *The English Carol* (London, 1958); Reginald Nettel, *Christmas and its Carols* (London, 1966); and *The Oxford Book of Carols*. For collections of folk carols, see Cecil Sharp, *English Folk-Carols* (London, 1911); R. Vaughan Williams, *Eight Traditional Carols* (London, 1919); and E. M. Leather and R. Vaughan Williams, *Twelve Traditional Carols from Herefordshire* (London, 1920).

Mary and Joseph,
Together did go,
And there they saw a cherry tree,
Both red, white and green.

Then up speaks Mary,
So meek and so mild:
O gather me cherries, Joseph,
For I am with child.

Then up speaks Joseph
With his words so unkind:
Let him gather thee cherries
That brought thee with child.

Then up speaks the little Child
In his own mother's womb:
Bow down, you sweet cherry tree,
And give my mother some.

Then the top spray of the cherry tree
Bowed down to her knee.
And now you see, Joseph,
There are cherries for me.

The house-to-house collection of money and gifts has long been associated with carol-singing. Cecil Sharp tells the story of how, when taking down songs from two old men, he asked if they knew a certain carol. One of the singers pleaded loss of memory, whereupon the other said, encouragingly: 'Stand up and think you've got snow in your boots and it'll come to you all right.' And it did!

A number of the pieces that we normally place under the heading of carols might more aptly be termed ballads, since

they are of a narrative nature. In fact, several are included in
Child, viz. 'St. Stephen and Herod' (22), 'Judas' (23), 'The
Cherry Tree Carol' (54), 'The Carnal and the Crane' (55),
and 'Dives and Lazarus' (56).

As in the ballad, some of the airs of the carol have a dance-
like quality, as in the example given below. And it is possible
that the forebears of the carol were associated with the
medieval *carole*, a dance-song.

Ex. 21

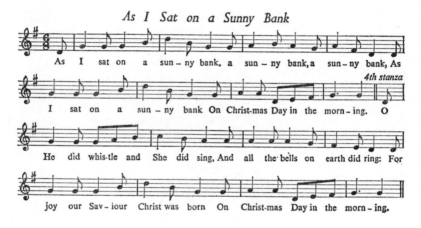

As I Sat on a Sunny Bank

As I sat on a sun-ny bank, a sun-ny bank, a sun-ny bank, As
I sat on a sun-ny bank On Christ-mas Day in the morn-ing. O
He did whis-tle and She did sing, And all the bells on earth did ring: For
joy our Sav-iour Christ was born On Christ-mas Day in the morn-ing.

I saw three ships come sailing by,
Come sailing by, come sailing by,
I saw three ships come sailing by
On Christmas Day in the morning.

And who d'you think were on the ship,
Were on the ship, were on the ship,
And who do you think were on the ship
But Joseph and his Fair Lady.

O he did whistle and she did sing,
For all the bells on earth did ring
For joy our Saviour Christ was born
On Christmas Day in the morning.

R. L. Greene, the great authority on the carol, has defined
it as 'a song on any subject, composed of uniform stanzas and
provided with a burden', which was the accepted definition
about 1550. By 'burden' he means 'an invariable line or
group of lines which is to be sung before the first stanza
and after all stanzas'. This definition does not, however,
apply to the traditional carol as we know it. The only manuscript carol of a date earlier than 1550 which has been found
in tradition appears to be the 'Corpus Christi Carol' or
'Down in yon Forest', though even here the introductory
burden is missing.

Ex. 22

Down in yon fo - rest there stands a hall, The bells— of Par - a - dise
I heard them ring, It's cov-er'd all o - ver with pur-ple and pall, And I
love my Lord Je - sus a - bove a - ny thing.

In that hall there stands a bed,
     The bells of Paradise I heard them ring,
It's covered all over with scarlet red,
     And I love my Lord Jesus above anything.

In that bed there lies a knight,
Whose wounds do bleed both day and night.

At the bedside there lies a stone,
Which the Sweet Virgin Mary knelt upon.

Under the bed there runs a flood,
The one half runs water, the other runs blood.

At the bed's foot there grows a thorn,
Which ever blows blossom since He was born.

Over that bed the moon shines bright,
Denoting our Saviour was born this night.

For the rest, the carols in Professor Greene's collection bear but little relationship to the traditional carol, though some may have a faint folk-song flavour.

Also classed as carols, and at times indistinguishable from them, are the songs associated with the ancient mid-winter custom of wassailing. This usually took place between Christmas and Epiphany. The word 'wassail' is thought to be of Saxon origin, *wes hál* ('be hale', or be of good health).

The wassail song may be sung on the house-to-house visit, or it may be performed in connection with the ceremony of apple-tree wassailing. The following example was noted by Cecil Sharp from a former 'wassailer' of Bratton, near Minehead.

Ex. 23

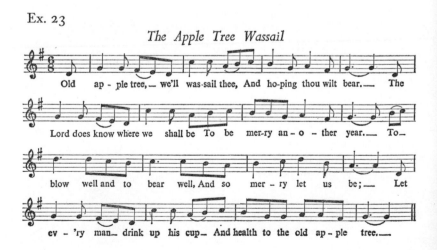

The Apple Tree Wassail

Old ap - ple tree, — we'll was-sail thee, And ho-ping thou wilt bear.— The Lord does know where we shall be To be mer-ry an - o - ther year.— To— blow well and to bear well, And so mer - ry let us be; — Let ev - 'ry man— drink up his cup— And health to the old ap - ple tree.—

Cecil Sharp did not see this particular ceremony, but it was thus described to him:

The wassailers would meet . . . in the orchard about seven or eight o'clock in the morning, join hands and then dance in a ring round an apple tree singing. . . . At the conclusion of the song, they stamped on the ground, fired off their guns and . . . shouted out in unison:

> Apples now, hatfulls, three-bushel bagfulls, tallets ole fulls, little heaps under the stairs.
> Hip, hip, hip, hooroo! (3 times)

They then placed some pieces of toast soaked in cider on one of the branches and proceeded to another tree, where the ceremony was repeated. When Cecil Sharp asked the singer what happened to the toast, he replied: 'All gone in the morning; some say the blackbirds eat it, but . . .'[5]

Cecil Sharp offers the explanation that the ritual is meant to propitiate the earth spirit and thus to ensure a good crop of apples in the next season.

Work-songs or occupation-songs of various kinds are common in many lands. They are described in this charming passage attributed to St. John Chrysostom, Bishop of Constantinople in the fourth century, who, in commenting on music in daily life, speaks about

nurses, who walking up and down singing, lull to sleep the eyelids of the babes in their arms; . . . waggoners who, driving their yoked animals at noon and singing to them, ease the hardship of the roads with their songs; . . . peasants who sing while cultivating their vines and gathering and treading their grapes; . . . sailors who sing while pulling at the oars; . . . women singing as they weave and separate the tangled threads.[6]

We have, however, to distinguish between songs which, according to Quintilian (c. A.D. 40 to 100), 'every troublesome and laborious occupation useth for solace and recre-

---

[5] See *Folk Songs from Somerset*, no. 128.
[6] Quoted by G. Reese, *Music of the Middle Ages*, p. 65 (New York, 1940).

ation' and those which on account of their rhythm and
construction directly assist in the performance of the particular work with which they are associated. It is only the
second category which are, strictly speaking, work-songs.

In England, the sea-chantey[7] or shanty (both the spelling
and the origin of the word are uncertain) is practically the
only work-song that has survived. With the substitution of
the steam-engine for sail in deep-sea craft even this is no
longer put to its traditional use, though a number of chanteys have been collected, many from retired chantey-men,
despite the rigid taboo (according to Stan Hugill) against
singing them on shore.

The chantey was never sung for entertainment, but only
in connection with work. It is performed by a soloist (the
chantey-man) and chorus. There are roughly two classes
of chantey: (1) The hauling chantey (called 'pulling chantey'
by Cecil Sharp) in which the physical effort is intermittent,
and (2) the heaving, or capstan, chantey, which is used to
accompany work of a regular, rhythmic nature, e.g. marching
round the capstan, working the pumps, etc.

Ex. 24

Sally Brown (Heaving Chantey)

I shipped on board of a Li-ver-pool li-ner, Way, ho, a-
rol-ling go; And I shipped on board of a Li-ver-pool li-ner
For I spent my mo-ney 'long with Sal-ly Brown.

[7] For collections, descriptions, and bibliographies, see Stan Hugill, *Shanties
from the Seven Seas* (London, 1961); Cecil Sharp, *English Folk-Chanteys* (London,
1914); R. R. Terry, *The Shanty Book* (London, 1921 and 1926); and W. B. Whall,
Sea Songs, Ships and Shanties (London, 1910).

O Sally Brown was a Creole lady.

O Sally Brown was a bright mulatto.

O seven years I courted Sally.

And now we're married and we're living nice and comfor'ble.

Ex. 25

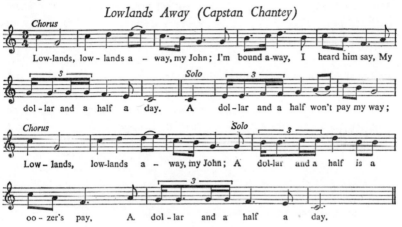

Lowlands Away (Capstan Chantey)

Chorus
Low-lands, low-lands a - way, my John; I'm bound a-way, I heard him say, My dol-lar and a half a day. A dol-lar and a half won't pay my way;

Solo

Chorus
Low-lands, low-lands a - way, my John; A dol-lar and a half is a oo-zer's pay, A dol-lar and a half a day.

Solo

A dollar and a half won't pay my way;
A dollar and a half is a white-man's pay.

We're bound away to Mobile Bay. (*bis*)

What shall we poor matelors do? (*bis*)

(According to John Short, a chantey-singer, an 'oozer' was a cotton stevedore, and 'matelors' meant sailors.)

There are other forms of work-songs in Scotland, e.g. the Gaelic waulking songs,[8] and it is possible that there were formerly other types in England. The only work-songs that

---

[8] See J. L. Campbell and Francis Collinson, *Hebridean Folksongs: A Collection of Waulking Songs* (Clarendon Press, Oxford, 1969).

appear to have survived (or have at least been noted), apart
from the sea-chanteys, are those of the Portland quarrymen whose songs were noted in 1954 by Peter Kennedy, to
whom I am indebted for information concerning them.
When working in the stone-quarries the men were accus-
tomed to improvise chants and songs as a means of obtaining
the rhythmic team-work required for their various jobs. In
the operation called 'reaming up', in which six or eight men
are employed in splitting up large squares of stone by means
of wedges, one of the songs they formerly used was called
'The French Tune' (see below). It is said that a French ship
had at one time gone aground off Portland Bill and that the
French sailors sang while they heaved on the 'jacks' to lift
the ship from the rocks. The quarrymen remembered the
tune and improvised the words in a supposed imitation of
the French (or possibly Basque) language.

Ex. 26

The hammers come down on the second and fourth beats
of the bar.

Nowadays 'The French Tune' is seldom sung, but the
men chant a patter that will give them the necessary rhythm,
or they sing songs and hymns with a suitable rhythm, such
as 'Parlez-vous', 'Abide with me', etc.

Street-cries might almost be included among occupation
songs, since they are used in connection with a trade, i.e.
to advertise wares for sale, but they are distinct from work-

songs in that they do not accompany the physical actions of the worker. Londoners (at least those of the older generation) will be familiar with the cry of the lavender-seller, but this is only one of the many cries that used to be heard in the streets of London and other cities.

Composers of the seventeenth and eighteenth centuries used the themes in madrigals, catches, etc. Handel is known to have taken great interest in London 'cries', and even jotted down a match-seller's cry on a loose sheet of paper.[9]

The street-cry is an example of the way in which all constantly reiterated utterances tend to take on rhythmic and melodic form. Usually it consists of a small thematic fragment, which is repeated with slight variations, as in this lavender cry noted by Cecil Sharp in the heart of London in 1908.

Ex. 27

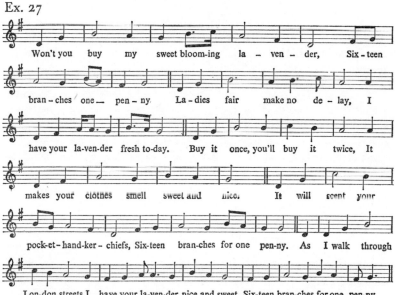

9 See *Journal of the Folk-Song Society*, vol. vi, pp. 55–72, for this and other street-cries, and for articles by Lucy Broadwood and Frank Kidson; also vol. iv, pp. 97–105 for further examples.

The following song noted in Kentucky was picked up from a Negro singer and has probably been developed from a street-cry:

Ex. 28

The Crow-Fish Man

Wake up, dar-ling, don't sleep too — late, The crow - fish man's done passed our gate, This morn-ing—— so soon.

> Selling crow-fish two for a dime,
> Nobody's crow-fish eats like mine,
> This morning so soon.

> Around the mountain I must go,
> If anything happens let me know,
> This morning so soon.

There is an amusing article entitled 'The Cries of London' by Addison in the *Spectator* of December 1711 in which he writes:

I must not omit one particular absurdity which runs through the whole vociferous generation. . . . I mean that idle accomplishment of crying so as not to be understood. Whether or no they have learned this from several of our affected singers, I will not take it upon me to say; but most certain it is, that people know the wares they deal in rather by their tunes than by their words; inasmuch that I have sometimes seen a country-boy run out to buy apples from a bellows-mender, and ginger-bread from a grinder of knives and scissors.[10]

The singing-game[11] is, like opera, a composite of singing, acting, and dancing. It is an ideal form of recreation for small children, and to the folklorist it is of interest as some of the games contain relics of ancient customs and beliefs. The musical themes on which children's singing-games

[10] *Spectator*, 1711, no. vi, pp. 51–4.
[11] The standard collection of English singing-games is A. B. Gomme, *The Traditional Games of England, Scotland, and Ireland* (London, 1894).

are built are very simple, and many are truly international. Themes such as the following are to be found over and over again in widely separated countries:

Instrumental dance-music is outside the scope of this book, but it is probable that many folk-dance tunes were originally song airs.[12] Sir Thomas Elyot in *The Boke called the Governour* (1531) writes of dances which take their names from 'the firste wordes of the dittie which the songs comprehendeth whereof the dance was made'.

There is a form of vocal dance accompaniment which should be mentioned, in which the singer uses wordless syllables. This is known as 'diddling', or 'deedling' in England, 'puirt-a-beul' or 'mouth music' in Scotland, 'lilting' in Ireland, and 'chin-music' in Newfoundland. The medieval prototype of this music may have been the *ductia*, which according to Johannes de Grocheo (*c.* 1300) was sung in ring dances by youths and maidens. He describes it as a textless piece, 'because although it may be performed by the human voice and represented by notes it cannot be set down by title [*per litteras*] since it does not have words or text'.[13] The rhythmic drive and vocal agility of some of these 'diddlers' is truly astonishing.

[12] A number of instances are given in Claude M. Simpson, *The British Broadside Ballad and its Music* (Rutgers University Press, New Jersey, 1966), and in articles by E. K. Wells entitled 'Playford Tunes and Broadside Ballads', in the *Journal of the EFDSS*, vol. iii, nos. 2, 3, and 4 (London, 1938–9).

[13] See Lloyd Hibberd, 'Estampie and Stantipes', in *Speculum*, xix, no. 2 (Cambridge, Mass., 1944), and J. Wolf, 'Die Musiklehre des Johannes de Grocheo', in *Sammelbände der Internationalen Musikgesellschaft* (1899–1900).

7

Broadsides and Early Collections

Though the tunes of the folk songs have been perpetuated almost entirely by oral transmission, the same is not equally true of the texts. These have been influenced by, or some may even owe their origin to, printed versions, particularly those which appeared in Broadsides.[1]

Broadside is the generic term for a single unfolded sheet, usually folio size, printed on one side only. It contained not only ballads and songs but proclamations, news, and many kinds of popular street literature. In fact, the broadside may be said to be the precursor of the popular press. It flourished from the middle of the sixteenth century onwards and died out only in the early years of the twentieth century. The first broadsides were printed in black-letter, or Gothic type, but this was discontinued about 1700.

We are here only concerned with the ballads and songs—broadside ballads, as they came to be termed. Over the centuries they were printed in their thousands. The Stationers' Company, which was incorporated in 1556, required the registration of ballads in the following year. Professor Hyder Rollins,[2] the great authority on early

---

[1] For further information about broadsides see Claude M. Simpson, *The Broadside Ballad* (Rutgers University Press, New Jersey, 1966); Leslie Shepherd, *The Broadside Ballad* (London, 1962), and *John Pitts* (London, 1967); G. Malcolm Laws, *American Balladry from British Broadsides* (Philadelphia, 1957); E. K. Wells, *The Ballad Tree*, Ch. 9; G. H. Gerould, *The Ballad of Tradition*, Ch. 9; Frank Kidson and Mary Neal, *English Folk Song and Dance*, Ch. 23 (Cambridge, 1915); and the works of Hyder E. Rollins.

[2] *An Analytical Index to the Ballad-Entries (1557–1709) in the Register of the Company of Stationers of London* (University of Carolina Press, reprinted Tradition Press, 1967). See also *A Pepysian Garland : The Black-Letter Broadside Ballads of the Years 1595–1639* (Cambridge University Press, 1922) and *Old English Ballads 1553–1625* (Cambridge, 1920).

broadside ballads, has listed over 3,000 in the register for the period 1557–1709, and this does not give a complete picture since there were many illegal presses, and many ballads were not registered. From 1641 their registration was not compulsory. In the eighteenth century broadside ballads were also printed in chapbooks, i.e. broadsides folded in booklet form.

In the nineteenth century, Seven Dials was the London centre of the broadside printing trade, and the broadsides that were printed reached astronomical numbers. It is said that during the early part of the century, London alone could boast of over fifty broadside printers. Of these James (Jimmy) Catnach, whose father had made engravings of Thomas Bewick's illustrations, was one of the best known. Others were John Pitts and H. P. Such. The latter, with his family, sold ballads from 1849 until as late as 1917.

Many broadsides have been preserved, though many more must have been lost, if only on account of the habit of pasting them on walls and cupboard doors, etc. Izaak Walton in *The Compleat Angler* (1653) speaks of 'an honest ale-house where we shall find a cleanly room, lavender in the window, and twenty ballads stuck about the wall'.

Fortunately various antiquaries have made collections of broadsides over the years. These include the Bagford and Roxburghe collections,[3] both in the British Museum; the Douce, Rawlinson, and Wood collections in the Bodleian Library, Oxford; and the great Pepys collection, started by Selden, in the Pepysian Library at Magdalene College, Cambridge, and several others in the University Library, Cambridge. An extensive collection, mostly from the nineteenth century, was made by the Reverend Sabine Baring-Gould and is deposited in the British Museum.

By no means all, or even the majority of, broadside ballads

---

[3] See *The Bagford Ballads*, ed. J. B. Ebsworth (1876), and *The Roxburghe Ballads*, ed. William Chappell and J. B. Ebsworth (1871–99), both published by the Ballad Society.

have a connection with folk song, though many have influenced it in one way or another. The broadside ballad emanated almost entirely from the cities and they were for the most part the work of ballad-mongers who sold them to the printers for a small sum. The ballad-maker would often peddle the broadsides around the countryside together with other wares, and he was wont to sing them himself to entice his customers. Such a pedlar was Autolycus in *The Winter's Tale*, who had 'songs for man and woman, of all sizes: no milliner can so fit his customers'. In the cities the broadsides were usually sold from a stall; hence the term 'stall ballad'.

During the reign of Queen Elizabeth, and the Commonwealth period, ballad singing was prohibited by law and ballad singers were liable to be punished, but it seems that they nevertheless continued to ply their trade.

The method of composition varied. At times the words of the ballad would be made up by the author and set to a popular tune; at others it would be a traditional song which he had picked up and which he or the ballad-printer would refurbish; and sometimes an unadulterated traditional song would reach the stage of printing.

The ballads in the first two categories had a deleterious effect on folk song. Some of the original compositions became popular and tended to oust the older traditional ballads; but probably the effect of the refurbished traditional ballads was even more harmful, for they had a confusing effect on the minds of the traditional singers, who, to be in the fashion, felt they must sing the songs in the new way. However, as Gerould says: 'There could be no better evidence of the vitality of folk song than the fact that it survived the cheapening and deadening effect of broadsides.'

The tunes of the folk song were not affected in the same way as the texts as, except for a short period at the end of the seventeenth century, they were not printed, and then usually in somewhat incomprehensible notation. In the oral tradition of the tunes there was, therefore, no interference and this is the main reason why most of the tunes that have come down to us are of a higher quality than the texts. On the other hand, the popularity of the broadside ballad had its compensations, for in helping to preserve the text, even though it might be in an inferior form, it helped to perpetuate the accompanying tunes.

It is probable that a large proportion of the texts of our English folk songs can be found on broadsides in one form or another, but there needs to be a good deal more research (on the lines of that undertaken in America by G. Malcolm Laws)[4] before we can speak with any certainty.

In the early eighteenth century a number of collections of popular songs were published, in which a few traditional songs were included. It is doubtful, however, whether these collections would have reached the traditional singers to any great extent, as did the broadsides. One with a wide circulation was *Wit and Mirth: or Pills to Purge Melancholy* (1719–20), edited by Thomas D'Urfey, the song-writer. This contains a number of popular songs, many from broadsides, as well as songs written by D'Urfey himself, which he set to ballad-airs, many of them being traditional. Another popular publication with a wide circulation was *A Collection of Old Ballads* (1723–5), thought to have been compiled by Ambrose Phillips. This contains a good proportion of genuine traditional ballads, but no tunes.

In Scotland there was Allan Ramsay's *The Ever Green* (1724), a collection of Scots songs said to have been written before 1600, and his *Tea-Table Miscellany* (1724–7) which contained about twenty popular ballads. Unfortunately the songs were assiduously polished as was so often the case in those days. In 1725 there appeared William Thomson's *Orpheus Caledonius*, the first song-book printed in Scotland which had tunes as well as words, though again there is very little traditional material.

---

4 *American Balladry from British Broadsides* (The American Folklore Society, 1957).

The event which created the greatest stir among literary circles was the publication in 1765 of *Reliques of Ancient Poetry* by Thomas Percy, afterwards Bishop of Dromore in Ireland. The circumstance which led to the publication of the *Reliques* was Percy's discovery, in the Shropshire home of his friend Humphrey Pitt, of a manuscript dating probably from the middle of the seventeenth century. This manuscript, which contained a number of ballads, was gradually being demolished by an unsuspecting housemaid to light the daily fires. Percy published a selection of the ballads (forty from a total of eighty) together with others taken from various manuscript collections and some ballads sent him by Lord Hailes. He did not hesitate to 'improve' the ballads and he presented them to the public in an apologetic manner, 'being sensible that many of these reliques of antiquity will require great allowances to be made for them'. The publication nevertheless aroused great interest both in England and on the Continent, and was an important element in the rise of the Romantic movement in literature. Wordsworth said: 'I do not think that there is an able writer in verse at the present time who would not be proud to acknowledge his obligation to the *Reliques*.'

Percy suffered a bitter attack from Joseph Ritson who both criticized his views on minstrelsy and castigated him for the editorial liberties he had taken—an attack that was strengthened by Percy's refusal to show the folio manuscript which contained the source of the ballads. It was not until one hundred years later, largely through the efforts of Professor Child, that the manuscript was bought, and was edited in full by J. W. Hales and F. J. Furnivall.[5]

Joseph Ritson's onslaught on Bishop Percy, though captious and ill-mannered, was no doubt born of conviction, for he was himself a scrupulous scholar. He edited several collections of ballads and songs emanating from both sides of the Border, the first of which, *A Select Collection of English*

---

[5] *Bishop Percy's Folio Manuscript* (London, 1867–8).

Tunes with their original airs, etc., appeared in 1783. Ritson was one of the first to appreciate the importance of the accompanying tunes, but, instead of finding traditional tunes in this collection, we get, to quote his own words, 'the production of the most eminent characters of the musical world'. 'Sigh no more ladies', with music by Arne, is an example. In fact, in this collection of English songs there are but few traditional texts, let alone tunes.

However, his *Scottish Songs* (1794) contains a fair proportion of traditional ballads and songs—both texts and tunes. These he took from manuscripts and printed sources. He admits that 'the genuine and peculiar natural song of Scotland is to be sought . . . in the production of obscure and anonymous authors, of shepherds and milkmaids . . . who were perhaps incapable of committing the pure inspiration of nature to writing'. And he gives a number of songs that he considers to have been so produced. Again, speaking of the tunes he believes that many were composed 'by shepherds tending their flocks, or by maids milking their cows; by persons, in short, altogether uncultivated'. Yet it seems not to have occurred to him to seek the songs from shepherds and milkmaids; indeed, he was mistrustful of tradition, describing it as 'a species of alchemy which converts gold to lead'.

With the exception of Percy and Ritson, most of the late eighteenth-century and early nineteenth-century compilers of old song collections were from Scotland. One of the most important was David Herd, whose *Ancient and Modern Scottish Songs*, etc., appeared in 1769, only a few years after Percy's *Reliques*, and ran through many editions.[6] To the title-page of the second edition (1796) are added the words 'Collected from Memory, Tradition and Ancient Authors'. One would suppose, therefore, that he collected songs from traditional singers, but he does not give his sources. Besides his published collections, he amassed a large

---

[6] See Hans Hecht, *Songs from David Herd's Manuscripts* (Edinburgh, 1904).

manuscript collection (now in the British Museum), on which subsequent collectors, including Burns and Scott, drew freely. Unfortunately Herd collected no tunes, but as regards the texts we may agree with Scott that it was 'the first classical collection of Scottish songs and ballads'.

To both Burns and Scott folk song owes an immeasurable debt of gratitude. Robert Burns (1759–96) was an ardent collector of folk songs, both words and tunes. Being of country origin, he acquired many songs during his early years. His outlet for these songs was the famous collection, *The Scots Musical Museum* (1787–1803). Though nominally edited by James Johnson, the collection owes much to the advice and assistance of Burns. He contributed many songs, both words and music, which he had recovered from oral tradition. In many cases, he re-worded the texts or used them as a basis for his own original compositions. In others he composed his own words to a traditional tune. So close was his creative poetic genius to the folk tradition that it is often difficult to disentangle his original work from the traditional material.[7] In the Preface to the first volume Burns wrote: 'Ignorance and Prejudice may perhaps affect to sneer at the simplicity of the poetry or music of some of these pieces, but their having been for ages the favourites of Nature's Judges —the Common People—was to the Editor a sufficient test of their merit.'

Burns then came to the aid of George Thomson in his compilation of *The Select Collection of Original Scottish Airs* (1793–1841).[8] Co-operation with Thomson was not so easy as with Johnson, as we may judge from the following lines written to Thomson by Burns: 'I have still several M.S.S. Scots airs by me, which I have pickt up, mostly from the singing of country lasses. They please me vastly; but your

[7] For references to the sources of Burns' songs, see James C. Dick, *The Songs of Robert Burns* (1903) and *The Songs and Poems of Robert Burns,* edited by James Kinsley (Clarendon Press, Oxford, 1968).

[8] The earlier volumes were reprinted several times with various additions and changes, including modifications of the title.

learned lugs [ears] would perhaps be displeased with the very feature for which I like them.'[9]

Pleyel, Haydn, and Beethoven were among those who made accompaniments for the songs. Thomson did not hesitate to change Burns' words and he even suggested alterations in the musical arrangements of Beethoven. Only Volume I was published during Burns' lifetime, though he had prepared songs for later volumes.

Burns was apparently not as interested in the ballads as in the lyrical songs. For the ballads we must look to Sir Walter Scott's *Minstrelsy of the Scottish Border* (1802–3), the most famous of all Scottish collections, though only of the texts. (Nine tunes were published posthumously by his son-in-law, J. G. Lockhart, in the 1833 edition of the *Minstrelsy*.) Scott was not content merely to delve into manuscripts and printed sources, but derived a great deal of his material from living oral tradition. Much of it was obtained in his early years from his 'raids' into Liddesdale and from his expeditions to the recesses of Ettrick Forest and the Vale of Yarrow.

He received a good deal of assistance from fellow scholars and collectors, including John Leyden, editor of *The Complaynt of Scotland* (see p. 48), Skene of Rubislaw, the compiler of a manuscript collection of thirty-two ballads which Scott called 'The Old Lady's Collection', and C. K. Sharpe, author of *The Ballad Book* (1823). Other friends who helped him were William Laidlaw and James Hogg, 'The Ettrick Shepherd', who contributed to the *Minstrelsy* a number of ballads which he had taken down from his mother's recital, or 'chaunt rather'. It was Hogg's mother, Margaret Laidlaw, who rebuked Scott, perhaps not undeservedly, with the oft-quoted words: 'There was never ane o' my sangs prented till ye prentit them yoursel' and ye hae spoilt them awthegither. They were made for singing an' no for reading,

---

[9] Quoted by David Daiches, *Robert Burns*, p. 327 (London, 1952), which should also be consulted for a general account of Burns' work.

but ye hae broken the charm now, and they'll never be sung mair.'[10]

Scott certainly did not 'spoil' the songs though he did not hesitate to 'edit' them, collating different versions and even adding lines of his own. In this he was not as successful as Burns, but he achieved his main object which was to present a number of readable texts and to arouse interest in the ballads.

Mention should be made here of the famous Mrs. Brown of Falkland,[11] to whom balladry will ever be grateful. Mrs. Brown, an intelligent and educated woman, had learned her ballads (of which nearly three dozen have been preserved) in childhood. She obtained them from her mother and an old nurse, but chiefly from an aunt who in turn had learned them from the singing of an old country-woman. Both Scott's *Minstrelsy* and Jamieson's *Popular Ballads and Songs* (1806), a rich repository of fine texts, contain ballads obtained from Mrs. Brown. Alas, neither Scott nor Jamieson gives her tunes.

Scott's enthusiasm was infectious and in the many years following the publication of the *Minstrelsy* many collections appeared.[12] The titles of the chief collections and their authors are given in the chronological list on page 109.

The year 1829 provided a landmark in ballad-collecting, for at that date there were published George Kinloch's *Scottish Ballads from Tradition* and William Motherwell's *Minstrelsy Ancient and Modern*. Both Kinloch and Motherwell collected from traditional sources, both were scrupulous in the presentation of the texts, and both gave a number of tunes which were noted by friends.

Motherwell's *Minstrelsy*, in addition to the beautiful

[10] James Hogg, *Domestic Manners of Sir Walter Scott* (1834).

[11] See 'Mrs. Brown and the Ballad', in Bronson, *The Ballad as Song*, for a biographical sketch, and a comparison of her manuscripts and consideration of the light that her variations throw on the composition of ballads.

[12] Further particulars of the collections will be found in Hustvedt, *Ballad Books and Ballad Men*—a most useful book.

ballads it contains, of which only a small number are non-traditional, has a most illuminating and readable Introduction in which he expresses full appreciation of the effectiveness of tradition in the preservation of the ballad. He says:

The tear and wear of three centuries will do less mischief to the text of an old ballad among the vulgar, than three short hours will effect, if in the possession of some sprightly and accomplished editor of the present day, who may choose to impose on himself the thankless and uncalled for labour of . . . trimming it from top to toe with tailor-like fastidiousness and nicety so as to make it fit for the press.

At the same time he excuses Percy's editorial practices on the grounds that there is a difference between the work that is intended for popular consumption and one that is addressed to the scholar. This is the view commonly held by later collectors in so far as the texts are concerned.

Peter Buchan, another Scottish collector of the early nineteenth century, has for long been under suspicion of having fabricated much of the material that he published, despite his assertion that 'the ballads are faithfully and honestly transcribed and given as taken down from the mouths of the reciters'. He has only recently been vindicated by Alexander Keith in his Introduction to Gavin Greig's *Last Leaves* (1925), of which we shall be speaking later.

We have so far been concerned with Scottish rather than English collections, for the simple reason that until the present century they were far more numerous. In any case, the study of English folk song would be incomplete if we did not take the Lowland Scots songs into consideration. Generally speaking, the area of distribution of the songs is determined by the language. Thus, the songs of Lowland Scotland are substantially the same as those of England, whereas they are entirely different from those of the Gaelic-speaking people of the Highlands and Islands. To quote Motherwell once again: 'It is difficult, if not impossible, to discriminate what truly may be considered as the native production of one or the other, i.e. the ballad poetry of England or Scotland.' (In this connection it is significant that Cecil Sharp called his collection 'Folk Songs *from* Somerset' and not *of* Somerset.) This does not mean that England had identically the same repertory of songs as Scotland. There are songs in Scotland that have not been found in England and vice versa. There are, too, differences between the Scottish and English vernacular. (Incidentally, in England there is far less use of local dialect in folk song than in speech and the same is, I understand, true of Scotland.)

Now, turning south of the border, the year 1843 marks another landmark in the collection of folk songs, for in that year there appeared the first publication in which all the songs were noted from traditional singers and all with their accompanying tunes. This was a volume of sixteen songs which were noted by the Reverend John Broadwood of Lyne, Sussex. The title-page, which is printed in an astonishing variety of types, gives an explicit description of the contents of the book, except that the collector modestly remains anonymous (see facing page).

His niece, Miss Lucy Broadwood, added ten songs to the collection and it was published in 1890 as '*Sussex Songs* arranged by H. F. Birch Reynardson', whose accompaniments were substituted for those of Mr. Dusart. Miss Broadwood gives this account of her uncle:

He was before his time in sympathising with the dialect, music and customs of country-folk. Family tradition describes the polite boredom with which his traditional songs, sung exactly as the smocked labourers sang, were received by his friends and relations. His accuracy of mind, excellent ear and real love for old things combined to make him a valuable pioneer. When Mr. Dusart, the Worthing organist, was asked to harmonize Mr. Broadwood's collection he made great outcries over intervals which shocked his musical standards. A flat seventh never *was*, and never *could* be! And so forth. To which it is recorded that Mr. Broadwood, confirming his intervals by vehement blasts on

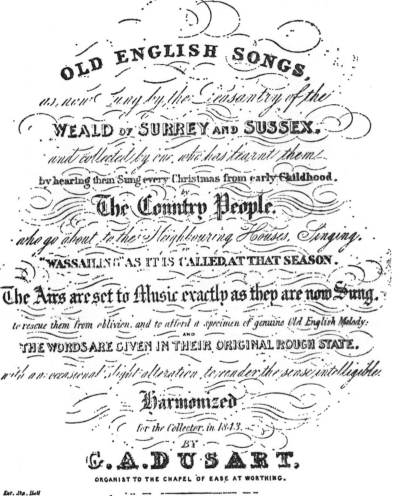

OLD ENGLISH SONGS,

as now Sung by the Peasantry of the

WEALD OF SURREY AND SUSSEX,

and collected by one, who has learnt them

by hearing them Sung every Christmas from early Childhood,

by

The Country People,

who go about to the Neighbouring Houses, Singing,

or "WASSAILING" AS IT IS CALLED, AT THAT SEASON.

The Airs are set to Music exactly as they are now Sung,

to rescue them from oblivion, and to afford a specimen of genuine Old English Melody:

AND

THE WORDS ARE GIVEN IN THEIR ORIGINAL ROUGH STATE,

with an occasional slight alteration, to render the sense intelligible.

Harmonized

for the Collector, in 1843,

BY

G. A. DUSART,

ORGANIST TO THE CHAPEL OF EASE AT WORTHING.

Ent. Sta. Hall

LONDON,

Published for the Collector, by BALLS & Cº 408. Oxford Street.

his flute, replied '*Musically* it may be wrong, but I *will* have it exactly as my singers sang it'.[13]

John Broadwood's collection does not appear to have had any immediate effect; it was rather the shadow cast by coming events. For it was some years before other collections with both text and tune taken 'from the mouths of the people' were published. It was not, in fact, until the end of the nineteenth or even the beginning of the twentieth century that the real campaign for the collection of songs began in England. This will be dealt with in the next chapter.

Three years after the appearance of John Broadwood's collection came James Henry Dixon's *Ancient Poems, Ballads and Songs of the English Peasantry*. Dixon evidently had a real appreciation of the circumstances of oral tradition, as witness this charming passage in the Preface:

He who travelling through the rural districts of England has made the road-side inn his resting place, who has visited the lowly dwellings of the villagers and yeomanry, and been present at their feasts and festivals, must have observed that there are certain old poems, ballads and songs which are favourite with the masses, and have been said and sung from generation to generation. Though for a time modern compositions may obscure their lustre, the new publications have only an ephemeral existence, and the peasantry go back to their antiquated favourites, remarking that 'the old rhymes are best, after all!'.

The 'rural districts' included the West Country as well as the Northern Dales, and a number of good traditional texts were gathered, but no tunes.[14]

These pioneers of field-collecting were followed by others, notably W. Christie, whose *Traditional Ballad Airs* was published in 1876 and 1881, and J. C. Bruce and J. Stokoe whose *Northumberland Minstrelsy* appeared in 1882. Both publications contain tunes. Many of those in Christie's collection are from Aberdeen, a rich territory, but un-

---

[13] *Journal of the Folk-Song Society*, vii, p. 81 (London, 1923).

[14] Dixon's work was reprinted with some additions by Robert Bell together with his *Early Ballads*, etc., in 1877.

fortunately his transcriptions are not always satisfactory. Some are an amalgam of different versions and in many cases he has added a second strain. *Northumbrian Minstrelsy* was instigated by a committee appointed by the Society of Antiquaries of Newcastle upon Tyne for the purpose of collecting the ancient melodies of Northumberland. The authors regretfully admit (as have others) that in their efforts to collect songs and ballads not already in print they were half a century too late. Notwithstanding, they obtained several from traditional singers, and in a few cases give the names of their informants.

William Chappell's *Popular Music of the Olden Time* (1855–9)[15] is justly esteemed as an invaluable source-book of old songs, but it is in no sense a compilation of folk songs. The texts and tunes have nearly all been taken from printed sources and hardly any are from oral recitation or singing. The songs, with copious and valuable notes, are grouped in chronological sections, dating from the reigns of King Henry VIII to Queen Anne, plus a section devoted to 'Traditional Songs of Uncertain Date', but this contains less than a dozen that we should regard as traditional in the sense of being 'of the folk', while there are about thirty traditional songs in the chronological sections. The airs are arranged with pianoforte accompaniments by Macfarren. *Popular Music of the Olden Time* was revised by H. E. Wooldridge under the title of *Old English Popular Music* in 1883, and not for the better. Incidentally, he omits the section 'Traditional Song'.

[15] Chappell should be consulted in conjunction with Claude M. Simpson, *The British Broadside Ballad and its Tunes* (Rutgers University Press, New Jersey, 1966).

8

The Folk Song Society and Later Collections

The compilers of the earlier collections described in the last chapter were, with a few exceptions, only incidentally concerned with the traditional aspects of the songs. Their interests were mainly antiquarian. Chappell's view, that only the printed verse or tune was trustworthy, was by no means uncommon; also the tunes were ignored by many collectors. At the end of the century[1] there was a change of emphasis. A new generation of collectors had arisen who concentrated their studies on the songs that they had obtained from living tradition, who noted the tunes and texts accurately, and who named their informants.

We have already mentioned the work of John Broadwood. Another pioneer—also a clergyman—was the Reverend Sabine Baring-Gould (1834–1924) of Lew Trenchard in Devonshire. Baring-Gould was not only the incumbent of the parish but also the squire—'squarson' as it used to be called. He had, therefore, unrivalled opportunities of getting to know the country-folk in the neighbourhood, and he was greatly beloved.

He was assisted in noting the melodies by the Reverend H. Fleetwood Shephard and the Reverend Dr. F. W. Bussell, Vice-Principal of Brasenose College, Oxford, but he had a good ear and was able to note a number of the tunes himself with the aid of a piano. He published *Songs and Ballads of the*

---

[1] A critical—one might say hypercritical—study of the collections and scholarly work of this period is given by D. K. Wilgus in *Anglo-American Folksong Scholarship since 1898* (Rutgers University Press, New Jersey, 1959). About half the book is concerned with the controversy about the communal origin of folk song.

West Country with accompaniments by Fleetwood Shephard in four volumes in 1889–92.[2]

In his Introduction Baring-Gould tells us that the airs are published precisely as noted, but admits that he has not been so scrupulous with the words. It is obvious at a glance that many passages are his own compositions. He excuses himself on the grounds that the original words were corrupt, fragmentary, or sometimes coarse, and he says, 'our object was not to furnish a volume for consultation by the musical antiquary alone, but to resuscitate and to popularize the traditional music of the English people'. In order to preserve a faithful record he deposited a copy of the songs as noted in the City Library of Plymouth. Baring-Gould's notes on the songs are very informative, for he was a scholar with a vast store of knowledge. He was a versatile and prolific writer. In addition to a large number of novels he wrote hymns ('Onward Christian Soldiers' is his best known) and many works on an assortment of subjects—religion, history, folklore, etc. His *English Minstrelsie: A National Monument of English Song* (8 volumes, 1895) exhibits a wealth of learning in its introduction and historical notes and indeed lives up to its title of 'a national monument'.

An event of far-reaching consequence was the inauguration of the Folk-Song Society[3] in 1898, which was formed (to quote from its rules) with the 'primary object of the collection and preservation of Folk-Songs, Ballads and Tunes, and the publication of such of these as may be deemed advisable'. From the beginning emphasis was laid on the music.[4]

---

[2] This was later revised and published in 1905 as *Songs of the West* under the musical editorship of Cecil Sharp with pianoforte accompaniments by H. Fleetwood Shephard, F. W. Bussell, and Cecil Sharp.

[3] For an account of the Folk-Song Society, see article by Frederick Keel, for many years its Honorary Secretary, in the *Journal of the EFDSS*, v, no. 3, p. 111 (1948).

[4] It enjoyed the support of many leading musicians. The first vice-presidents were Sir John Stainer and Charles Stanford, Professors of Music at the Universities

The Society instigated no systematic plan for the collection of songs, but depended on the voluntary efforts of its individual members. Its main activity was to publish an annual Journal containing songs collected by its members with annotations by an editorial committee. In 1899, the year after the formation of the Society, a slim number of the Journal was published which contained Sir Hubert Parry's inaugural address, together with other addresses and eleven songs noted mainly by Mrs. Kate Lee, the Honorary Secretary. During the next three years three more numbers were published, accounting for another 110 tunes. Then the Society lapsed into inactivity, probably mainly on account of the illness and subsequent death of its Honorary Secretary. Largely due to Cecil Sharp's importunities, it came to life again in 1904, and its continued activities were ensured by the appointment of Miss Lucy Broadwood as Honorary Secretary and Cecil Sharp as a member of the committee.

The Journal continued until 1932, when the Society amalgamated with the English Folk Dance Society to become the English Folk Dance and Song Society. It produced eight volumes (35 numbers) which form an unsurpassed treasure-house of English folk song. In addition to songs, it contains a number of valuable articles. After amalgamation the Journal was named the *Journal of the English Folk Dance and Song Society*, and for many years was edited by Frank Howes. In 1965 the title was changed to *Folk Music Journal*.

Of the many contributors to the *Journal of the Folk-Song Society* only a few can be mentioned here.[5] The greatest of all collectors was Cecil Sharp, of whom we shall be speaking

---

of Oxford and Cambridge respectively, Sir Alexander Mackenzie, Principal of the Royal Academy of Music, and Sir Hubert Parry, Director of the Royal College of Music. In the first list of the Society's members appear the names of Edward Elgar, H. Plunket Greene, W. H. Hadow, Joseph Joachim, and many other musicians.

[5] A list of the principal contributors is given on pp. xiv–xv of the *Index* to the Journal, edited by Margaret Dean-Smith.

later. He contributed to four numbers of the Journal (one posthumously). Next to him, Vaughan Williams[6] probably did more than any one to bring folk song to the notice of the public. This he did by his writings, his lectures, and, above all, by his beautiful arrangements. He was an assiduous collector and noted over 800 tunes (including variants). These included a number of carols noted in Herefordshire in conjunction with Mrs. E. M. Leather. It is of interest that he collected his first folk song, the lovely 'Bushes and Briars' (see overleaf) at Ingrave, Essex, in December 1904, only three months after Cecil Sharp had started to collect in Somerset. Though they were great friends, it was some time before Vaughan Williams mentioned his discovery to Cecil Sharp for, with typical modesty, he was afraid of boring him!

The two who contributed most to scholarship in the pages of the Journal and elsewhere were Miss Lucy Broadwood (1858–1929) and Miss Anne Geddes Gilchrist (1864–1954). To Miss Broadwood the Folk-Song Society owes more than to any other individual.[7] For many years she was its Honorary Secretary, for a time editor of its Journal, and finally its President. She was an accomplished musician and was endowed with a fine sense of scholarship. Her various articles and notes on the songs were invaluable. She collected many songs herself and in conjunction with Fuller Maitland. It was largely through her wise administration that the Society held together and prospered.

Anne Gilchrist, though never a member of the committee, served for many years on its editorial board and contributed copious notes and articles to the Journal. She had a wide knowledge of history and folklore, and a fund of out-of-the-way information concerning ancient customs, which were

---

[6] See 'Folk Song and Nationalism', Ch. 3, in Michael Kennedy, *The Works of Ralph Vaughan Williams* (London, 1964).

[7] See articles by R. Vaughan Williams and F. Howes in the *Journal of the English Folk Dance and Song Society*, vol. v, no. 3, p. 136 (London, 1948).

Ex. 29

Bushes and Briars

Through bu-shes and through bri. – ars. I late-ly took my— way; All—
for to— hear the small birds sing, And the lambs to—
skip and play; ———— All— for to— hear the
small birds sing, And the lambs to —— skip and— play.

I overheard my own true love,
Her voice it was so clear;
Long time I have been waiting for
The coming of my dear.

Sometimes I am uneasy
And troubled in my mind;
Sometimes I think I'll go to my love
And tell to him my mind.

And if I should go to my love,
My love he will say Nay;
If I show to him my boldness,
He'll ne'er love me again.

all brought to bear on the elucidation of living folk song and
dance. Her knowledge of tunes was prodigious, and many
a scholar has been relieved of the tedious business of tracing
a tune by the simple expedient of writing to 'Aunt Anne',

as she became known on both sides of the Atlantic. Always a reply came by return giving the desired information, and a wealth of other knowledge that the inquiry had aroused in her memory. There could never have been a more generous scholar or one who sought the limelight less. It is typical that she never published a book or collection of songs apart from her contributions to the Journal.

Of Frank Kidson (1855–1926) it has been said that his antiquarian interest made him, musically speaking, a lineal descendant of William Chappell. His knowledge was wide-ranging, as witness the many entries that he supplied to Grove's *Dictionary of Music and Musicians*, but his most important work was *British Music Publishers* (1900). His *Traditional Tunes* (1891), according to Miss Broadwood, 'marks a turning-point in the history of folk-song, for it is the first book of English traditional songs in which tunes and texts, given in "undoctored" form, are accompanied by scholarly critical notes'.[8]

Percy Grainger (1882–1961), the composer and brilliant pianist, made a unique contribution to folk song. In its scientific study and in his methods of collection he was well ahead of his time. He was one of the first to use the phonograph (a Standard Bell model) on any extensive scale in collecting. This enabled him to make a close analysis of the singing style of the performers.[9] His articles in the *Journal of the Folk-Song Society*, vol. iii, no. 12 (1908) on 'Collecting with the Phonograph' and 'Impress of Personality on Traditional Singing', together with the transcription of some of the songs he collected, throw a flood of light on the subject. He published no collections of folk song apart from his contribution to the *Journal of the Folk-Song Society*, but a

[8] See *Journal of the Folk-Song Society*, vol. viii, p. 48 (1927), and also *Journal of the English Folk Dance and Song Society*, vol. v, no. 3, p. 127 (1948).

[9] His original cylinders are located at the Grainger Museum, Melbourne, Australia, and copies are at the Music Division, Library of Congress, Washington, D.C., and the British Institute of Recorded Sound, 29 Exhibition Road, London S.W.7. (See also record, 'Unto Brigg Fair', LEA 4055.)

number arranged with pianoforte accompaniment have appeared separately under the general title of 'British Folk Music Settings'. Percy Grainger is best remembered by the general public for his arrangement of the Morris dance-tunes, 'Shepherd's Hey' and 'Country Gardens', both col-lected by Cecil Sharp, but he made a number of other beauti-ful folk-song settings. In addition to English folk songs he collected many from Denmark in collaboration with Ewald Tang Christensen. Other pioneers were W. P. Merrick, who as early as 1901 contributed to the *Journal of the Folk-Song Society* fifty-two songs that he had noted from a single singer; Henry E. D. Hammond and his brother Robert who made a large collection in Dorsetshire; and G. B. Gardiner whose field was Hampshire. Gardiner secured the collaboration of Vaughan Williams, Balfour Gardiner, and others in noting the tunes.

George Butterworth (1885–1916), a composer of great promise, was one of the most valued workers in the field of folk song and folk dance. Unhappily he was killed during the First World War at the early age of thirty-one. Coming under the influence of Vaughan Williams and Cecil Sharp, he started collecting folk songs in 1908 and later co-operated with Cecil Sharp in the collection of Morris dances. His first encounter with folk music was disturbing, for it made him realize the artificiality of much of his early work (which he destroyed), but later he found, as did Vaughan Williams, that the folk music idiom provided him with a language in which he could freely express the musical ideas which came to him. The few compositions he has left are entrancingly beautiful, particularly his song cycle, *A Shropshire Lad*, and *The Banks of Green Willow* for small orchestra, the latter being based on a folk song of that name.

Another composer of a later date who contributed to the *Journal of the Folk-Song Society* was E. J. Moeran (1894–1950). He was drawn to folk song from hearing it from the village singers in Norfolk where his father was vicar, and it was he who persuaded The Gramophone Company to record that fine traditional singer, Harry Cox.

All the collectors we have mentioned, save Miss Gilchrist, have published separate collections of the songs independently of the Folk-Song Society. Particulars are given in the Bibliography on pages 111–12. In the *Journal of the Folk-Song Society* the songs were published scrupulously as noted, except for the occasional omission of lines that, at that time, were considered too free for publication (see p. 53). In the collections that were published for general use, and not primarily for scholarly study, it was often found necessary to repair missing or corrupt lines. This patching was in most cases done with discrimination, though one must admit that some of the earlier editors allowed their gifts of literary composition too free a hand. Baring-Gould has already been mentioned in this connection, and Charles Marson, who was responsible for editing the texts in the earlier volumes of *Folk Songs from Somerset*, was another offender. When the songs were republished Cecil Sharp remedied most of Marson's indiscretions.

The editing of texts is a delicate task which can only be done successfully by keeping to the folk-song idiom and where necessary collating different versions of the text. Most of the recent collectors have adopted this principle. With the tunes there was no tampering and these were always published as noted. Collectors would endeavour to get as many variants as possible and then select the best for publication.

Most of the collections published during the first half of the present century are presented with pianoforte accompaniments. Ideally the songs should be sung unaccompanied, but at the time the only way of getting them accepted by the uninitiated was to provide accompaniments for, to the general public, melody dissociated from harmony was unthinkable. In contrast to the situation today, there were few homes in England, however humble, that did not possess a piano. Many of the tunes have harmonic implications and it is possible for a perceptive and sensitive musician to harmonize them without doing violence to their nature, provided always that he keeps the tune in the forefront of his mind and does not use it merely as a medium for his own musical invention.

Many musicians whom we have already mentioned, namely Vaughan Williams, Cecil Sharp, Gustav Holst, George Butterworth, and Percy Grainger, have enhanced the songs by their settings, providing as it were a frame for the picture. This list is by no means complete and, in addition to piano accompaniments, many beautiful part-song and choral arrangements have been made by Vaughan Williams, Gustav Holst, and others.

During the first years of the century, when collecting in England was proceeding apace, and even earlier, the county of Aberdeenshire was yielding up its treasures. This was due to Gavin Greig (1856–1914), who with Cecil Sharp was perhaps among the last of the great collectors. From 1879 until his death, he was schoolmaster at Whitehill in the parish of New Deer, Aberdeenshire, and it was shortly after his appointment that he started to collect ballads and songs. In this he was assisted by the Reverend J. B. Duncan. Their entire collection consists of over 3,000 texts with slightly more tunes. For three and a half years Gavin Greig conducted a folk-song 'corner' in the *Buchan Observer*, to which correspondents were invited to send texts of folk songs. This was printed as *Folk Songs of the North East*. At the time of his death he and the Reverend J. B. Duncan were engaged on a project to publish the tunes they had collected together with the texts, restricting themselves first to ballads. After Greig's death in 1914 the editing was continued by Duncan, who unhappily died three years later. The work was then taken over by Alexander Keith and to him we owe the magnificent collection entitled *Last Leaves of Traditional Ballads and Ballad Airs* (1925). The work contains 108 Child ballads (about 250 tunes and 125 texts). Both texts and tunes are of considerable interest. About one-third of the tunes are in the pentatonic scale and nearly half are hexatonic, while most of the remaining tunes are basically hexatonic or pentatonic. *Last Leaves* can be numbered among the classic collections of British folk ballads.

9

Cecil Sharp and Recent Field Work

'The greatest dynamic in the folk-song world.' It was thus that Gavin Greig, the Aberdeenshire collector, addressed Cecil Sharp. Cecil Sharp (1859–1924)[1] was not, as we have seen, the first English folk-song collector, nor by any means the only one, but he towered above his fellows in the extent of his collection. With others the collection and study of folk music was a side-line, but with Cecil Sharp it was a vocation to which he dedicated the last twenty-one years of his life.

Though he was no mean scholar, it was chiefly the artistic aspect of folk song that appealed to him. He was a professional musician, who among other musical activities had been director of the Music Conservatoire at Hampstead (now no more) and a music-teacher at Ludgrove Preparatory School. He did not start collecting folk songs until 1903 when he was over forty years of age, though his interest in folk music had been aroused some years earlier when he by chance saw the traditional Morris Dancers at Headington, near Oxford.

The story has many times been told of the 'discovery' of his first folk song. It was in the little village of Hambridge in Somerset, when staying with his friend, the Reverend Charles Marson, that he heard the vicarage gardener, appropriately called John England, singing to himself as he mowed the lawn. The song was the now well-known 'Seeds of Love'.

---

[1] Only a slight sketch of his work will be given here as a full account can be read in *Cecil Sharp: His Life and Work* by Maud Karpeles (London, 1967).

Ex. 30

My garden was planted well
With flowers ev'rywhere;
And I had not the liberty to choose for myself
Of the flowers that I love dear. (*bis*)

The gard'ner was standing by;
And I asked him to choose for me.
He chose for me the violet, the lily and the pink,
But those I refused all three. (*bis*)

The violet I did not like,
Because it blooms so soon.
The lily and the pink I really overthink,
So I vow'd that I would wait till June. (*bis*)

In June there was a red rosebud,
And that is the flow'r for me.
I oftentimes have pluck'd that red rosebud
Till I gained the willow tree. (*bis*)

The willow tree will twist
And the willow tree will twine.
I oftentimes have wish'd I were in that young man's arms
That once had the heart of mine. (*bis*)

Come all you false young men,
Do not leave me here to complain;
For the grass that has oftentimes been trampled under foot,
Give it time, it will rise up again,
Give it time, it will rise up again.

This simple song from the lips of a living singer brought home to Cecil Sharp, as no song from a printed collection had ever done, the real significance of the folk-song tradition. It revealed to him the existence of a world of natural musical expression to which everyone, no matter how humble nor how exalted, could lay claim by virtue of his common humanity.

From then on he devoted every available moment to collecting the songs, and shortly afterwards the dances, and making them known. He succeeded in gathering nearly 5,000 tunes (of which nearly one-third were from the Southern Appalachian Mountains of America) and many dances. He lost no time in bringing out a selection of the songs he had collected.[2] The first of the five volumes of *Folk Songs from Somerset* was published in 1904 in co-operation with Charles Marson, who edited the texts of the first three volumes.

But publication was not enough. With the zeal of a missionary he set about making the songs known, not merely to scholars but to people in all walks of life. This he did largely through illustrated lectures which he gave up and down the country, and through his campaign in the public press. He realized, however, that if the practice of folk song was to become nation-wide it must be introduced into the schools, and it was in no small measure due to his persistent persuasion, and the publication of a cheap series of folk songs for schools, that the songs eventually found their way into the educational curriculum.

[2] See Karpeles, *Cecil Sharp*, p. 108. A definitive edition of his English folk-song collection is in the press.

This was not achieved without conflict with the education authorities and also with his fellow-members of the Folk-Song Society. In 1905 the Board of Education issued a Blue Book in which it recommended the teaching of folk songs in schools and added a list of suggested songs in which hardly a single genuine folk song appeared. Sharp rose immediately to the challenge and in the daily press he hotly disputed the claim of these so-called 'national' songs to be regarded as folk songs. Though the members of the Folk-Song Society's committee were in general agreement with Cecil Sharp's views, few, with the exception of Vaughan Williams, were prepared to support him in his uncompromising attack on the action of the Board of Education. He may at the time have seemed to be unnecessarily pedantic, and perhaps lacking in diplomacy, but it was to him all-important that from the outset the distinction should be recognized between the song composed by the individual and that which had been evolved by countless generations of singers. This campaign in the press attracted great public attention, but the most beneficial outcome of the controversy was that it persuaded Cecil Sharp to give expression to the faith that was within him by writing *English Folk Song: Some Conclusions* (first published 1907).

Some of his fellow-workers tended to look askance at his activities. Despite their published collections intended for general use, they were still inclined to regard folk songs as museum pieces which might become tarnished were they too freely exposed to popular taste.

By the beginning of the present century, when Cecil Sharp and others were actively searching for songs, the tradition was fast disappearing, or at least going underground. There were many reasons for this. The disruption of village community life, the growth of industrialism, and the increase of literacy all played a part. The sudden collapse of agriculture in the 1870s had as its consequence (to quote G. M. Trevelyan) 'the general divorce of Englishmen from life in contact with nature, which in all previous ages had helped to form the mind and imagination of the island race'.[3] Cecil Sharp and other collectors have confirmed that most of their songs were obtained from people over the age of sixty. The old people still loved the songs, but they had allowed them to recede into the background of their memories owing to the lack of appreciation by younger members of the community. These 'old songs' had for the time being gone out of fashion and the singers were shy and fearful of being met with ridicule. So the songs did not come readily to mind and it required tact and patience to obtain them.

Cecil Sharp often wished he had been born at an earlier age when English folk song was in its prime, and it seemed almost a miracle when in a sense that wish was fulfilled. In the Southern Appalachian Mountains of America he found the collector's paradise.[4] He spent forty-six weeks in the mountains during the years 1916–18 together with the present writer, and we collected nearly 1,600 tunes, including variants.

The mountain regions of North Carolina, Tennessee, Virginia, and Kentucky are inhabited by people whose ancestors left the British Isles some two hundred years previously. Until recently they had been more or less cut off from the rest of the world on account of the mountainous nature of the country. Fifty years ago, when we were there, there were few roads: just rough tracks over the mountains or alongside the rivers, or even at times in the river-bed itself. The mountain people lived in small, more or less self-contained communities, for the most part in primitive log-cabins. They scratched the soil and provided for their own subsistence. Few could read or write, but they had a fine inherited culture and this was nowhere more apparent than

---

[3] *English Social History*, p. 553.

[4] See Sharp/Karpeles, *English Folk Songs from the Southern Appalachians*; and *Cecil Sharp*, Chs. XII and XIII.

in their songs: folk songs of British origin. Everyone sang them, old and young alike, and they sang little else. In fact, throughout our stay in the mountains we never heard a bad tune, except occasionally when we were staying at a missionary settlement.

We had the delightful experience of living in a really musical atmosphere. Imagine the thrill of coming without warning on this beautiful version of 'Edward'.

Ex. 31

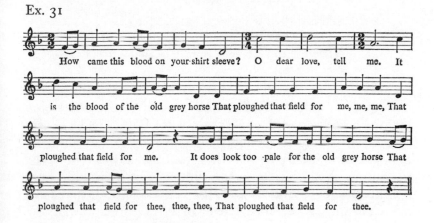

How came this blood on your shirt sleeve?
 O dear love, tell me.
It is the blood of the old greyhound
That traced that fox for me, me, me,
 That traced that fox for me.
It does look too pale for the old greyhound
That traced that fox for thee, thee, thee,
 That traced that fox for thee.

How came this blood on your shirt sleeve?
 O dear love, tell me.
It is the blood of my brother-in-law
That went away with me, me, me,
 That went away with me.

And it's what did you fall out about?
  O dear love, tell me.
About a little bit of bush
That soon would have made a tree, tree, tree,
  That soon would have made a tree.

And it's what will you do now, my love?
  O dear love, tell me.
I'll set my foot in yonder ship
And I'll sail across the sea, sea, sea,
  And I'll sail across the sea.

And it's when will you come back, my love?
  O dear love, tell me.
When the sun sets into yonder sycamore tree,
And that will never be, be, be,
  And that will never be.

A good proportion of the tunes are cast in the pentatonic scale. There are two possible reasons for this. (1) The ancestors of many of the people hailed from the Lowlands of Scotland, and it may be that their folk music was cast in the pentatonic mode owing to the influence of their Highland neighbours; or (2) more likely, the pentatonic scale may have been current in the folk music of both England and the Scottish Lowlands in earlier times. It would need much research to solve the problem if, indeed, it can ever be solved.

Alas, the ideal state of affairs that Cecil Sharp and I found in 1916–18 has not persisted. The country has been opened up, roads have been built, and the serpent in the guise of radio and records has pentrated this Garden of Eden. I made two return visits in 1950 and 1955 and I found that the children of most of our former singers no longer sang their parents' songs.

The Appalachian Mountain region was unique in the number of beautiful folk songs that it produced, but it was by no means the only part of America in which folk songs of English origin were, and still are, to be found. Many fine collections of folk songs have been made in other parts of the United States and in Canada. Over and over again one is led to marvel at the indestructibility of tradition.

After Cecil Sharp's death in 1924 there was but little collecting in England until 1952 when the British Broadcasting Corporation organized a systematic recording campaign. It secured the services of a number of collectors, among whom were Peter Kennedy and Seamus Ennis, the latter working mainly in Ireland. It would not have been surprising had there been but little to be found after the country had been so thoroughly scoured by Cecil Sharp and his contemporaries, but though few entirely new songs were discovered, many variants turned up and considerably enriched the store of traditional material. In all some 1,600 items were recovered.[5]

The 'pleasant drudgery' of collecting (to quote Motherwell) was considerably eased by the tape-recording machine which came into common use by the middle of the present century. Recording by mechanical means, beside ensuring accuracy, gives a reproduction of the singer's style which no written notation can do.

The collectors did not restrict themselves to England, but explored also Scotland and Ireland, where the tradition was found to be more alive than in England. We have already spoken of the common folk-song language of England and Scotland, and the same is true of Ireland, where folk songs in the English language exist, as they do in Scotland, side by side with those of the Gaelic-speaking people. English folk songs were probably carried into Ireland from the time of the Cromwellian Settlements from the mid-seventeenth century onward,[6] but it is doubtful if they would have had a wide currency until the nineteenth century when English became the dominant language of the Irish people.

With the decline of Irish as a spoken language, the people

[5] Copies of these have been deposited in the Vaughan Williams Memorial Library at Cecil Sharp House.

[6] See Donal O'Sullivan, *Songs of the Irish* (Dublin, 1960).

had recourse to the making of songs in English, often to the accompaniment of a tune that had previously been associated with Gaelic words. These new 'Anglo-Irish' songs, including those that originally came from England and Scotland, have for many generations been transported to England with the constant influx of Irish labour (see also p. 55). The first representative collection of Anglo-Irish folk songs was P. W. Joyce's *Old Irish Folk Music and Songs* (1909) and it has been succeeded by a number of other collections.

In Wales, where the native language has been to some extent retained, only a small number of English folk songs has been recovered, though some fine songs have come from the Gower Peninsula, an English-speaking region of Wales, and others will be found in the pages of the *Journal of the Welsh Folk Song Society* (founded in 1908).

In addition to the field-work organized by the B.B.C., the systematic collection of folk song in Scotland (Lowlands as well as Highlands) has been undertaken since 1951 by the School of Scottish Studies, Edinburgh University. Collecting is also being carried on in England and Ireland, though perhaps on a less organized basis than in Scotland.

Folk Song in the Present Day

The corpus of English folk song has now been collected, though stray songs, mostly variants, still turn up and will continue to do so. Often in the foregoing pages with their account of early collections one has become impatient at the thought of opportunities missed: the poring over manuscripts when the living tradition was at hand, the 'improvement' of texts, and, above all, the neglect of the tunes. But instead of bemoaning what we have lost, let us rather be thankful for what we have. Slowly and surely collectors have come to realize the real nature and significance of the folksong tradition. Thanks to their pioneer work, we are now in possession of a vast store of treasure which has been preserved for all time in the form of manuscripts, printed collections, and, latterly, recordings. Never before has such a varied wealth of material been available, which can at any moment be turned into living song.

And our gratitude must go to the traditional singers who have treasured the songs in their memories. Paradoxically, in some ways the very agents that have helped to destroy the traditional practice of folk singing are now to some extent ministering to its revival. The bearers of the tradition, who had put aside their songs because they felt them to be no longer in the fashion, have had their confidence restored by hearing them over the radio and on gramophone records, and by seeing them in print. This was exemplified by a singer in North Carolina who said: 'When I forget Mother's songs, I know I have only to look at Cecil Sharp's book, and they will come back to me just exactly right.'

Nevertheless, with the transference from oral to visual habits one cannot expect the preservation and evolution of folk song to continue indefinitely by the old traditional methods, so it is well that we have permanent records of the songs to which traditional and non-traditional singers alike can have access. One can appreciate the sentiments of a folk singer who, after her songs had been recorded, exclaimed: 'How wonderful to think that my songs will now live on when I am no longer here!'

It is sometimes questioned whether folk songs which arose in social conditions so dissimilar from those that prevail at the present time can have a living appeal for this and coming generations. The answer is that a folk song is a work of art and like any other art it stands or falls on its intrinsic merits. The works of Purcell and Bach do not become out of date because they were written in times different from our own, and the same is true of folk songs. The best of them, like the classics, have a fundamental quality which enables them to outlive passing fashions and ways of life.

The folk-song revival is not an antiquarian movement— a sentimental endeavour to put back the clock—nor even an attempt to provide an artificial form of escapism, like the pastoral diversions of Marie Antoinette. Far from being a museum piece, folk song, as we know, is having a wave of popularity. It is being communicated by the agencies of the mass media, and there is an ever-growing number of 'folk clubs', 'folk groups', and 'folk singers'. At the same time we have to recognize that this very popularity has brought in its train certain practices which have tended to obscure the distinctive qualities of folk song.

In its popular presentation folk song suffers all too often from a crude and insensitive accompaniment which has the effect of blunting its characteristic melodic and rhythmic features. Folk song will lend itself to many kinds of treatment and an instrumental accompaniment, as we have seen, is not in itself necessarily detrimental, provided that it is of a kind that emerges from the song itself and is not super-imposed upon it.

On the other hand, in the few instances that the songs are

sung unaccompanied, the performer is inclined to give a superficial imitation of the traditional singer's manner of singing, which produces an artificial effect somewhat akin to the adoption of rustic speech by a townsman. The singer of folk songs has everything to gain by studying the art of the good traditional singer,[1] but he will not be master of that art until he has absorbed the songs into his innermost being. Imitation is not enough.

It is rare, at the present time, for a concert singer to include folk songs in his repertory. In fact, the opinion (a kind of inverted snobbery) is often expressed that folk song lies outside his competence. This is, of course, a fallacy. The trained singer can interpret folk song as well as anyone else provided that he uses his skill to serve the needs of the song and does not treat it as a medium for the display of his vocal talents. Folk song is not the prerogative of any one type of singer, but, whether he be professional or amateur, the singer must live with the song long enough to discover its inner meaning if he is to do it justice. Simplicity of expression must not be mistaken for insignificance of content.

More harmful than the inadequate presentation of the songs is the misuse of the word 'folk', which is to be seen in the present habit of attributing the term 'folk song' to any popular, or would-be popular, song that is composed in what is thought to be a folk-style. This is not merely an academic question. It goes to the heart of the matter, for nothing is so likely to debase the currency as the issue of counterfeit coins.

One is not, of course, suggesting that creative effort should be curbed. On the contrary, the revival of folk song, as we have already seen, has had a fertilizing effect on individual creation; but, however good the composition of an individual may be, it is different in character from folk music which, being the product of countless generations, does not bear an individual imprint. Therefore, to attach

[1] See Discography, p. 115.

the term 'folk song' to a newly composed song, besides being erroneous, is injurious to the conception of folk song.

It is often suggested that, given time, a newly composed song may become a folk song, as indeed it has in the past. But this is hardly possible in present circumstances, for nowadays immediately a song becomes current it is stereotyped by means of print or gramophone record, and no matter how popular it becomes or how often it is picked up by ear, it can always be referred back to the original. Thus its development is stultified.

For the same reason the evolution of genuine traditional folk songs has also been checked to a very great extent. But we are convinced that the best will continue to be enjoyed in the form in which they have come down to us on account of their inherent beauty. We have to distinguish between the *making* and the *practice* of folk songs. In the past the two processes were inseparable, but that is no longer the case. Though we may no longer be able to make folk songs in the present day we can still enjoy singing them.

We have to recognize that not every version of a folk song is a great work of art, for there have been bunglers as well as artists among the folk. So now, as when the songs were perpetuated by oral transmission, selection will play its part. Happily we have at our disposal a rich and varied repertory of beautiful songs from which to choose.

As this book shows, we know all too little about the origins and history of folk song. It would seem that at the beginning of the century the English folk-song tradition was almost the exclusive monopoly of one small section of the community. For how long that had been so, we cannot say with certainty, but there are indications that the tradition was formerly more widespread. However that may be, thanks to Cecil Sharp and other collectors, our glorious heritage of folk song, which had been preserved in the obscurity of country cottages, can now become the possession of every English man, woman, and child.

Sources of Musical Examples

ABBREVIATIONS

JFSS: *Journal of the Folk-Song Society*

Karpeles *Newfoundland*: Maud Karpeles, *Folk Songs from Newfoundland*. Faber & Faber 1971.

Karpeles *15 FSN*: Maud Karpeles, *15 Folk Songs from Newfoundland* with pf. acc. by R. Vaughan Williams. London 1934.

Sharp *Appalachian*: Cecil Sharp edited Maud Karpeles. *English Folk Songs from the Southern Appalachians*. London 1960 [1932].

Sharp *Carols*: Cecil Sharp, *English Folk-Carols*. Novello 1911.

Sharp *Cent.*: Cecil Sharp, *English Folk Songs* Centenary Edition. Novello 1960. (Published as Selected Edition, 1920.)

Sharp *Chanteys*: Cecil Sharp, *English Folk-Chanteys*. Simpkin & Marshall 1914.

Sharp *FSEO*: Cecil Sharp, *Folk Songs of English Origin collected in the Appalachian Mountains*. Novello 1920.

Sharp *FSS*: Cecil Sharp, *Folk Songs from Somerset*. Simpkin 1909.

Sharp *MDT*: Cecil Sharp, *Morris Dance Tunes*. Novello 1907–24.

Vaughan Williams *Carols*: R. Vaughan Williams, *Eight Traditional Carols*. Stainer & Bell 1919.

Vaughan Williams *FSEC*: R. Vaughan Williams, *Folk-Songs from the Eastern Counties*. 1908. Republished in *English County Songs*, Novello 1961.

1 The Cuckoo (p. 4)
    (*a*) Noted by Cecil Sharp
    (*b*) Karpeles *Newfoundland* p. 245 and Karpeles *15 FSN* p. 42
    (*c*) Sharp *Appalachian* ii version C p. 180 and Sharp *FSEO* ii p. 45
2 The Unquiet Grave (p. 6)
    (*a*) Sharp *Cent.* ii p. 18
    (*b*) Noted by Cecil Sharp

3   Come all ye fair and tender Ladies (pp. 8 and 9)
       Sharp *Appalachian* ii
       (*a*) Version D p. 130
       (*b*) Version P p. 135
       (*c*) Version E p. 130
       (*d*) Version A p. 128 and *FSEO* i p. 33
4   Fair Margaret and Sweet William (p. 10)
       Sharp *Appalachian* i p. 132
5   The Maid of the Mill (p. 17)
       (*a*) William Shield, *Rosina* (1783)
       (*b*) Sharp *MDT* v p. 4
       (*c*) Sharp *MDT* v p. 6
6   Searching for Lambs (p. 22)
       Sharp *Cent.* i p. 74
7   Barbara Ellen (p. 24)
       Sharp *Cent.* i p. 20
8   The Banks of Sweet Dundee (p. 25)
       Noted by Cecil Sharp
9   The Keys of Canterbury (p. 27)
       Sharp *Cent.* ii p. 110
10 As I walked out (p. 27)
       Vaughan Williams *FSEC* p. 16 (*English County Songs* p. 58)
11 My Bonny Bonny Boy (p. 28)
       Sharp *Cent.* i p. 82
12 The Wraggle Taggle Gypsies (pp. 33 and 34)
       (*a*) Sharp *Cent.* i p. 13
       (*b*) Noted by Cecil Sharp
13 Henry Martin (p. 34)
       (*a*) Noted by Cecil Sharp
       (*b*) Sharp *Cent.* i p. 1
14 The Nightingale (p. 36)
       Sharp *Appalachian* ii version E p. 194 and Sharp *FSEO* ii
       p. 88
15 As I walked through the Meadows (p. 37)
       Sharp *Cent.* i p. 88
16 Lord Rendal (p. 42)
       Sharp *Cent.* ii p. 2
17 The Coasts of High Barbary (p. 44)
       Sharp *Cent.* i p. 32

Grateful acknowledgements are given to Novello & Co., Oxford University Press, Stainer & Bell, and Faber & Faber for permission to quote songs from their publications and also to the agent of the Cecil Sharp Estate.

Bibliography

This bibliography gives a selection of the more important publications. Fuller bibliographies are contained in some of the works cited. References to particular aspects of the subject are also given in the footnotes. Readers are particularly recommended to consult *A guide to English folk song collections 1822–1952, with an index to their contents, historical annotations and an introduction* by Margaret Dean-Smith (The University Press of Liverpool, 1954).

Many of the works referred to, as well as manuscript collections and gramophone records, can be consulted at the Vaughan Williams Memorial Library at Cecil Sharp House, 2 Regent's Park Road, London N.W.1.

A SELECTION OF WORKS ON ENGLISH FOLK SONG

Bertrand Harris Bronson, *The Ballad as Song*. Berkeley, California, 1969.
> A collection of essays.

Gordon Hall Gerould, *The Ballad of Tradition*. Oxford, 1932. (Reprinted 1960.)

Frank Howes, *Folk Music of Britain—and Beyond*. London, 1969.

Maud Karpeles, *Cecil Sharp: His Life and Work*. London, 1967.

A. L. Lloyd, *Folk-song in England*. London, 1967.

Cecil J. Sharp, *English Folk Song: Some Conclusions* (1907). 4th edition, edited Maud Karpeles, London, 1954. (Facsimile reprint, E. P. Publishing Ltd., 1972.)

Evelyn K. Wells, *The Ballad Tree*. New York, 1950.

Iola A. Williams, *English Folk-Song and Dance*. London, 1935.
> A short but very readable account of the subject.

R. Vaughan Williams, *National Music and Other Essays*. London, 1963.
> The essays under the heading 'National Music' (first published 1934) are concerned with folk music.

A SELECTION OF PUBLISHED COLLECTIONS

(* = contains tunes)   († Reprinted 1961 in *English County Songs*)

1719–20   Thomas D'Urfey, *Wit and Mirth or Pills to Purge Melancholy*. London.*

1723–5   *A Collection of Old Ballads*, etc. London.

1724   Allan Ramsay, *The Ever Green*, being a Collection of Scots Poems written by the ingenious before 1660. Edinburgh.

1724–7   Allan Ramsay, *The Tea-Table Miscellany*, etc. London.

1725   William Thomson, *Orpheus Caledonius*. London.*

1765   Thomas Percy, *Reliques of Ancient English Poetry*, etc. London. 1866 edition by H. B. Wheatley, reprinted by Dover Publications, New York, 1966.

1769   David Herd, *Ancient and Modern Scottish Songs, Heroic Ballads*, etc. Edinburgh.

1783   Joseph Ritson, *A Selection of English Songs with their Original Airs*, etc. London.*

1787–1803 James Johnson, *The Scots Musical Museum*. Edinburgh.*

1790   Joseph Ritson, *Ancient Songs and Ballads from the Reign of King Henry the Second to the Revolution*. London. Reissued by the Singing Tree Press, Detroit, 1968.

1793–1841 George Thomson, *A Select Collection of Original Scottish Airs*, etc. Edinburgh and London.* (See note on p. 74.)

1794   Joseph Ritson, *Scottish Songs*. London.*

1795   Joseph Ritson, *Robin Hood*. London.

1802–3   Walter Scott, *Minstrelsy of the Scottish Border*, etc. Revised and edited by T. F. Henderson, 1932 (9 tunes published in an Appendix to 1833 edition). Reissued by the Singing Tree Press, Detroit, 1968.

1806   Robert Jamieson, *Popular Ballads and Songs from Tradition, Manuscripts and Scarce Editions*, etc. Edinburgh.

1810   R. H. Cromek, *Remains of Nithsdale and Galloway Songs*, etc. London.

1822   Davies Gilbert, *Some Ancient Christmas Carols with the Tunes to which they were formerly sung in the West of England*. London.*

1823   Charles Kirkpatricke Sharpe, *A Ballad Book*. Edinburgh.

1825   Allen Cunningham, *The Songs of Scotland*. London.

1825   Peter Buchan, *Gleanings of Scotch, English and Irish Scarce Old Ballads,* etc. Peterhead.

1827   George R. Kinloch, *The Ballad Book.* Edinburgh.

1827   George R. Kinloch, *Ancient Scottish Ballads recovered from Tradition,* etc. London.*

1827   William Motherwell, *Minstrelsy, Ancient and Modern,* etc. London.* Reissued by the Singing Tree Press, Detroit, 1968.

1828   Peter Buchan, *Ancient Ballads and Songs of the North of Scotland,* etc. Edinburgh.

1833   William Sandys, *Christmas Carols, Ancient and Modern including the most popular in the West of England,* etc. London.*

1834   *The Universal Songster, A Museum of Mirth,* etc. London.

1843   John Broadwood, *Old English Songs,* etc., harmonized by G. A. Dusart. London.* Collection added to by Lucy Broadwood and published [1890] as *Sussex Songs* with accompaniments by H. T. Birch Reynardson.

1846   James Henry Dixon, *Ancient Poems, Ballads and Songs of the Peasantry of England,* etc. London. Revised and enlarged edition by Robert Bell, London, 1857 and 1877.

1850   Edward F. Rimbault, *Musical Illustrations of Bishop Percy's Reliques of Ancient English Poetry,* etc. London.*

1855-9   William Chappell, *Popular Music of the Olden Time,* etc. London.* Reissued by Dover Publications, New York, 1965.

1856   Robert Bell, *Early Ballads illustrative of History, Tradition and Customs.* London. (See also 1877.)

1864   William Allingham, *The Ballad Book,* etc. London.

1867-8   John W. Hales and Frederick J. Furnivall, *Bishop Percy's Folio Manuscript, Ballads and Romances.* London. Reissued by the Singing Tree Press, Detroit, 1968.

[1868]   William Henry Husk, *Songs of the Nativity,* etc. London.*

1876-81   W. Christie, *Traditional Ballad Airs,* etc. Edinburgh.*

1877   Robert Bell, *Early Ballads together with Ancient Poems, Ballads and Songs.* London. (See 1846 and 1856.) Reissued by the Singing Tree Press, Detroit, 1968.

[1877]   M. H. Mason, *Nursery Rhymes and Country Songs, both tunes and rhymes from tradition.* London.*

1882–98   Francis James Child, *The English and Scottish Popular Ballads*. Boston.* (55 tunes.) See also Bronson 1959–72. Reprinted by Dover Publications, New York, 1965.

1882   John Collingwood Bruce and John Stokoe, *Northumbrian Minstrelsy: A Collection of the Ballads, Melodies and Small-Pipe Tunes of Northumbria*. Newcastle upon Tyne.* Reissued by Folklore Associates, Hatboro, Pennsylvania, 1965.

1888   Heywood Sumner, *The Besom Maker and other Country Folk-Songs*. London.*

1889–92   Sabine Baring-Gould, *Songs and Ballads of the West Country: A Collection made from the Mouths of the People* with H. Fleetwood Shephard. London.* Revised edition, 1891–5. See also *Songs of the West*, 1905, which contains omissions, additions, and changes.

1891   William Alexander Barrett, *English Folk Songs*. London.*

1891   Frank Kidson, *Traditional Tunes: A Collection of Ballad Airs*, etc. Oxford.* Facsimile reprint by S. R. Publishers, Wakefield, Yorks., 1970.

1893   Lucy E. Broadwood and J. A. Fuller-Maitland, *English County Songs*. London.*

1899   Robert Ford, *Vagabond Songs and Ballads of Scotland*. Paisley and London.* (A few tunes.)

1899–1931 *Journal of the Folk-Song Society*. London.*

1904–9   Cecil J. Sharp, *Folk Songs from Somerset*. Taunton.* 5 vols. (vols. 1 to 3 with Charles L. Marson). Many of the songs are published elsewhere—see *Novello's School Songs*, 1908–25, and *English Folk-Songs* (Selected Edition), 1920.

1905   S. Baring-Gould, *Songs of the West*, with H. Fleetwood Shephard and F. M. Bussell under the musical editorship of Cecil Sharp. London.* (Reprinted 1913.) A revised edition of *Songs and Ballads of the West Country*, 1889–92 and 1891–5.

1905   Lucy Broadwood, *English Traditional Songs and Ballads*. London.*

1908–25   Cecil J. Sharp, 116 songs in *Novello's School Songs* series (which contains also 11 by Vaughan Williams and 9 by

Hammond). Most of the songs are included in other publications. London.*

1908   H. E. D. Hammond, *Folk-Songs from Dorset*.† London.*

1908   Ralph Vaughan Williams, *Folk Songs from the Eastern Counties*.† London.*

1909   George B. Gardiner, *Folk Songs from Hampshire* with pf. acc. by Gustav Holst.† London.*

1909   P. W. Joyce, *Old Irish Folk Music and Songs*. London.*

1910   Alice E. Gillington, *Old Christmas Carols of the Southern Counties*. London.*

1911   Cecil J. Sharp, *English Folk Carols*. London.*

1911   W. Percy Merrick, *Folk Songs from Sussex*.† London.*

1912   Cecil J. Sharp, *Folk Songs from Various Counties*.† London.*

1913   George Butterworth, *Folk Songs from Sussex*. London.*

1914   Cecil J. Sharp, *English Folk Chanteys*. London.*

1915   Clive Carey, *Ten English Folk Songs*. London.*

1919   Ralph Vaughan Williams, *Eight Traditional Carols*. London.*

1920   E. M. Leather and R. Vaughan Williams, *Twelve Carols from Herefordshire*. London.*

1920   Cecil J. Sharp, *English Folk Songs*. Selected Edition. London.* Many of the songs are included in *Folk Songs from Somerset*, 1904–9, and *Novello's School Songs*, 1920–5. Republished in Centenary Edition, 1959.

1921   W. Gilles Whittaker, *North Countrie Ballads, Songs and Pipe Tunes*, etc. London.*

1921–26   R. R. Terry, *The Shanty Book*. London.*

1923   Alfred Williams, *Folk Songs of the Upper Thames*. London. Reissued by the Singing Tree Press, Detroit, 1968.

1924   E. J. Moeran, *Six Folk Songs from Norfolk*. London.*

1925   Alexander Keith, *Last Leaves of Traditional Ballads and Ballad Airs collected in Aberdeenshire by the Late Gavin Greig*. Aberdeen.*

1932   E. J. Moeran, *Six Suffolk Folk Songs*. London.*

1932–64   *Journal of the English Folk Dance and Song Society*. London.* A continuation of the *Journal of the Folk-Song Society*, 1899–1931.

1959   R. Vaughan Williams and A. L. Lloyd, Ed., *The Penguin Book of English Folk Songs.* London.*

1959–72 Bertrand Harris Bronson, *The Traditional Tunes of the Child Ballads with their Texts according to the Extant Records of Great Britain and America.* Princeton.*

1961   R. Vaughan Williams, Ed. Imogen Holst and Ursula Vaughan Williams, *A Yacre of Land.* London.*

1965   Frank Purslow, Ed., *Marrow Bones,* English Folk Songs from the Hammond and Gardner Mss. London.*

1965   *Folk Music Journal.* London.* A continuation of the *Journal of the English Folk Dance and Song Society,* 1932–64.

1968   Percy Grainger, Ed. Patrick O'Shaughnessy, *Twenty-one Lincolnshire Folk Songs.* London.*

SOME AMERICAN COLLECTIONS CONTAINING FOLK SONGS OF ENGLISH ORIGIN WITH TUNES

Phillips Barry, Fanny Hardy Eckstorm, Mary Winslow Smyth, *British Ballads from Maine.* New Haven, 1929.

B. M. Belden, *Ballads and Songs collected by the Missouri Folk-Lore Society.* Missouri [1940], 1955.

Frank C. Brown, *Collection of North Carolina Folklore.*
 Vol. II. *Folk Ballads from North Carolina,* 1952.
 Vol. III. *Folk Songs from North Carolina,* 1952.
 Vol. IV. *The Music of the Ballads,* 1957.
 Vol. V. *The Music of the Songs,* 1962.   North Carolina.

Helen M. Creighton, *Songs and Ballads from Nova Scotia.* Toronto, 1932. Reissued by Dover Publications, New York, 1966.

Maritime Folk Songs. Toronto, 1961.

Arthur Kyle Davis Jr., *Traditional Ballads of Virginia.* Cambridge, Mass., 1929.

More Traditional Ballads of Virginia. Chapel Hill, 1960.

Helen Hartness Flanders, *Ancient Ballads traditionally sung in New England.* Philadelphia, 1960–5.

Edith Fowke, *Traditional Singers and Songs from Ontario.* Hatboro, Pennsylvania, 1965.

Emelyn Elizabeth Gardner and Geraldine Jencks Chickering, *Ballads and Sea Songs of Southern Michigan.* Ann Arbor, 1939. Reissued Hatboro, Pennsylvania, 1967.

Elisabeth Bristol Greenleaf and Grace Yarrow Mansfield, *Ballads and Sea Songs from Newfoundland*. Cambridge, Mass., 1933. Reissued Hatboro, Pennsylvania, 1968.

Maud Karpeles, *Folk Songs from Newfoundland*. London, 1971.

MacEdward Leach, *Folk Ballads and Songs of the Lower Labrador Coast*. Ottawa, 1965.

Kenneth Peacock, *Songs of the Newfoundland Outports*. Ottawa, 1965.

Vance Randolph and Floyd C. Shoemaker, *Ozark Folk Songs*. Columbia, Missouri, 1946–50.

Dorothy Scarborough, *A Song Catcher in Southern Mountains*. Columbia, 1937.

Cecil J. Sharp and Maud Karpeles, *English Folk Songs from the Southern Appalachians*. London [1933], 1960.

LOCATION OF MANUSCRIPTS OF COLLECTIONS REFERRED TO IN CHAPTER 8

S. Baring-Gould: City of Plymouth Public Library.

Lucy Broadwood: Cecil Sharp House.

George Butterworth: Cecil Sharp House.

Clive Carey: Cecil Sharp House.

G. B. Gardiner: Cecil Sharp House.

Anne Gilchrist: Cecil Sharp House.

Percy Grainger: Copy of 300 songs collected in Lincolnshire at Cecil Sharp House.

Gavin Greig and J. B. Duncan: The library of King's College, Aberdeen. Microfilm copy at Cecil Sharp House.

H. E. D. and R. Hammond: Cecil Sharp House.

Frank Kidson: Mitchell Library, Glasgow. Some photostat negatives at Cecil Sharp House.

E. M. Leather: Cecil Sharp House.

W. P. Merrick: A few songs at Cecil Sharp House; the rest in private possession.

Cecil Sharp: Clare College, Cambridge. A microfilm copy at Cecil Sharp House. Photostat copies at Harvard University Library and the New York Central Library.

R. Vaughan Williams: British Museum. A copy at Cecil Sharp House.

Note: Manuscripts housed at Cecil Sharp House are in the Vaughan Williams Memorial Library, Cecil Sharp House, 2 Regent's Park Road, London N.W.1.

Discography

The following is a short, by no means complete, list of traditional singers whose style of unaccompanied singing is particularly recommended. In addition, there are many good individual items in the ten volumes of the Folk Songs of Britain series: Topic 12T 157–61 and 12T 194–8, originally issued by New York Caedmon TC 142–6, TC 163–4, and TC 124–5.

It should be borne in mind that some of the singers were past the prime of life and that in consequence their voices have suffered.

ENGLISH AND SCOTTISH

* EFDSS Classics are available only to members and associates of the English Folk Dance and Song Society.

George Belton	EFDSS Folk Classics 1008*
Bob Copper	
For 'The False Bride', the only solo song on the record.	Topic 12T 157
Harry Cox	EFDSS Folk Classics 1004*
Harry Cox	DTS LFX 4
Lizzie Higgins. In 'The Travelling Stewarts'	Topic 12T 179
Fred Jordan	
Particularly 'John Barleycorn'	Topic 12T 150
Norman Kennedy	
Scots Songs and Ballads	Topic 12T 178
Joseph Leaning. In 'Unto Brigg Fair'	Leader LEA 4050
Jeannie Robertson	
'Jeannie Robertson, The Great Scots Traditional Singer.'	Topic 12T 96
Her *chef d'œuvre*, not included in the above, is 'My Son David'	HMV DLP 142
Also in 'The Travelling Stewarts'	Topic 12T 179
Phoebe Smith	Topic 12T 193

Belle Stewart. In 'The Travelling Stewarts'	Topic 12T 179
Cathie Stewart. In 'The Stewarts of Blair'	Topic 12T 138
Jane Stewart. In 'The Travelling Stewarts'	Topic 12T 179
Sheila Stewart. In 'The Stewarts of Blair'	Topic 12T 138 and
and 'The Travelling Stewarts'	Topic 12T 179
Phil Tanner	EFDSS Folk Classics
Particularly 'Henry Martin', 'The Gower Wassail', 'The Gower Reel', 'The Sweet Primroses'.	1005*
Above titles also issued on	Col. CA 1605
'Henry Martin', also on	Topic 12T 161
Joseph Taylor. In 'Unto Brigg Fair'	Leader LEA 4050

IRISH

Packie Byrne	EFDSS Folk Classics 1009*
Sarah Makem (Ulster ballad singer)	Topic 12T 182
Peg Clancy Power	Folk Legacy FSE 8
Paddy Tunney	Folk Legacy FSE 7
Paddy Tunney: 'A Wild Bees' Nest'	Topic 12T 139
Paddy Tunney: 'The Irish Edge'	Topic 12T 165

AMERICAN AND CANADIAN

Horton Barker	Folkways FA 2362
Particularly 'Lord Thomas and Fair Ellinor', 'The Turkish Rebilee', and 'There was an old Lady'.	
Tom Brandon (the singer is of Irish descent)	Folk Legacy FSC 10
Dillard Chandler. In 'Old Love Songs and Ballads from the Big Laurel, N.C.', particularly 'Matthy Groves'.	Folkways FA 2309
Frank Profitt	
For 'Song of the Lost Hunter' ('Young Hunting'). The rest of the songs are accompanied.	Folk Legacy FSA 1

Index